Wondering

Christianity for Questioners

DAVID FEDDES

Christian Leaders Press
Monee, Illinois
christianleadersinstitute.org

Wondering: Christianity for Questioners
Copyright © 2017 David Feddes
Published by Christian Leaders Press
Monee, Illinois
www.christianleadersinstitute.org

Printed in the United States of America

Cover images from Shutterstock
Cover design by Jaclyn Feddes

ISBN: 0692799044
ISBN-13: 978-0692799048

CONTENTS

A World of Wonders

Imagine waking up some morning to see the sun rising in the west. The water in a nearby river is flowing uphill. Beside the river are trees on which pizzas are growing. An elephant flies overhead. A bull strolls past, guided by a radar system. Mice walk along following directions on a map.

How would you react? Wouldn't you be astonished? But think about the world we're in. Is it any less amazing than the world we've just imagined?

Is it any less amazing for the sun to rise in the east than in the west? We watch the sun come up in the east, and we take it for granted. We explain it in terms of which way the earth spins. But who says the earth has to spin that way? Why couldn't it reverse and spin the opposite way? We might answer "inertia," but what is inertia? It's just a label. It's a word for the mysterious fact that things tend to keep doing whatever they're doing, but it does absolutely nothing to explain that fact.

Is it any less amazing for water to flow downhill than uphill? What makes water flow downhill? We might say "gravity," but what kind of answer is that? Again, it's just a label, not an explanation. It doesn't tell us where this force called gravity comes from or why it pulls downward instead of pushing upward. Why be amazed at a fantasy that some hidden force would make water flow uphill and not be amazed at the real-life fact that a mysterious force we've labeled gravity pulls water downhill?

Why be amazed at the thought of trees making pizzas and not be amazed that trees make apples and oranges? For that matter, why not be amazed that people make pizzas?

Why be any more astonished at flying elephants than flying eagles and bumblebees and airplanes? Why marvel at the fantasy of a radar-equipped bull and be bored with the reality of radar-equipped bats? Why be shocked at the notion of mice following maps, but yawn when salmon follow internal maps to their spawning grounds and when migrating birds navigate thousands of miles to a precise destination?

We live in a world that's as full of marvels as a fairy tale. It might be amazing for a frog to become a prince, but isn't it just as amazing for a tadpole to become a frog?

Our world is full of wonders that are meant to make us wonder. Wondering may mean questioning; it may also mean marveling. The best sort of wondering does both. Wondering involves a sense of curiosity and a sense of awe. In wondering, we ask "How?" and exclaim "Wow!"

If you have hard questions that demand reasonable answers, Christianity addresses your mind. If you feel amazed at the marvels and mysteries of life, Christianity expands your spirit. This book explores how sensible and stunning Christianity is, in case you were wondering.

Chapter One

Physical Evidence of the Creator

Antony Flew was one of the world's leading atheists. While teaching at Oxford and other universities, he wrote many articles and books arguing against belief in God. He took the atheist side in many public debates. But after decades of making a case for atheism, Flew gave up. He said that he must "go where the evidence leads." The evidence pointed to a Creator of enormous intelligence and power.

What changed his mind? "Recent scientific discoveries," explained Flew. New knowledge of cell complexity and genetic coding persuaded Flew that life required intelligent design. Even the simplest cell is so complex that it's almost impossible to see how the first living thing could have emerged by chance. Flew said, "What I think the DNA material has done is show that intelligence must have been involved."

Intelligent Design

Each human cell contains enough DNA information to fill at least 1,000 books of 500 pages each. Could such information be encoded and transmitted by an accidental process? If you found a library containing half a million pages of information, would you assume it was all written by accident without any intelligent author? It would take a huge leap of faith to believe such a thing.

Francis Crick won a Nobel Prize for his discoveries in the structure of DNA. After studying genetic codes, Crick did not think that random evolution could ever produce DNA from scratch. So did he conclude that God was involved? No, instead he said that perhaps aliens from outer space sent primitive life forms to earth in a spaceship, and things evolved from there. For him, almost any theory would be better than admitting that God is real. Still, Crick knew the information embedded in DNA had to originate with some kind of superior intelligence, although his commitment to atheism kept him from crediting that intelligence to God.

Living cells are marvels of design. Molecular biologist Michael Behe writes, "The cell is essentially a completely automated factory, so all assembly has to be done by highly sophisticated robots, not by magic." If a single cell can be compared to a factory with robots, imagine the complexity of a body made up of billions of cells and the kind of information needed to produce such a body.

Behe speaks of "irreducible complexity." By this he means something that can't even begin to work until all of its parts are present and working together. Behe uses a mousetrap as an example. You can't take part of a mousetrap, such as the wooden base, and catch a few mice, then add a spring and catch a few more, add a hammer and catch a few more, and so on. The mousetrap needs to be designed and built with each part in place and connected to the other parts before it can catch its first mouse. In the same way, an irreducibly complex system in the body must be assembled all at once before it can do its job. It can't appear gradually, piece by piece.

An example of this is the eye. The eye has a lens, an adjustable focus, light sensors, a variable diaphragm which controls the amount of light, and so forth. No part can do its job unless the other parts of the eye are also present. Charles Darwin's evolutionary theory claimed natural selection as the force that drives evolution without any designer. However, living things that evolved only some parts of an eye would have no adaptive advantage over their relatives. The various parts of an eye would be useless in natural selection until all parts were present and working together. Darwin himself wrote, "When I think of the eye, I shudder. To suppose that the eye could have been formed by natural selection seems absurd in the highest degree."

Darwin didn't know the half of it. In his time, little was known about biochemistry. The more we discover about what's inside the organs and cells of living things, the more complex and intricate the design turns out to be. It's easier to believe that mousetraps evolve by accident than to believe that complex organs and cells and biochemical processes evolved by accident. Even the simplest living cell requires over 200 complex enzymes. British scientist Sir Fred Hoyle estimated the likelihood of those 200 enzymes being produced and combined by chance as 1 with 40,000 zeroes behind it. Hoyle said that life popping into existence by chance was as improbable as a tornado blowing through a junkyard and producing a jet aircraft.

Could living things come from dead matter as the result of a purposeless process? Has anyone ever observed such an event? Never. In fact, scientists have completely discredited spontaneous generation, the notion that living things spring up from dead matter. It never happens. Scientists and educators know this. Yet some cling to their faith that somehow, long ago, spontaneous generation did take place, that dead matter did somehow produce living things. Scientists have run all kinds of experiments, trying to produce a living cell from non-living material. They've spent a great deal of research, time, and money trying to show how it could happen. They still haven't succeeded.

But just suppose they eventually did succeed. Suppose they somehow produced a living cell from dead matter. What would that prove? That life is an accident, with no creator or intelligent designer? Far from it! Obviously, any life form that resulted from many decades of work by thousands of scientists would be the product of intelligent design, not proof that life evolved by accident. Meanwhile, no such experiment has worked. If so many brilliant scientists still haven't been able to produce even the simplest life form from non-living matter, doesn't it make sense to conclude that it would take someone with power and intelligence far greater than ours to design and create the fantastically complex forms of life that we see on our planet?

Atheist Faith Commitment

You might get the impression from some experts and educators that if you stick to facts and evidence, you won't believe in God. If you're smart, you'll realize that the world and all its creatures come from a natural process, not from a Creator. The National Association of Biology Teachers issued a statement declaring that all life arose by an "unsupervised, impersonal, unpredictable, and natural process." A widely used biology textbook insists, "Evolution is random and undirected... without either plan or purpose." A leading encyclopedia states that natural selection is "automatic, with no room for divine guidance or design."

This is not a conclusion based on evidence; it is a faith commitment. It takes a lot of faith to believe that the universe and everything in it came into being without a Creator. With evidence of design and complexity all around them, atheists trust in the miraculous powers of chance, and they take a leap of faith. By faith they believe that nothing produced something, randomness produced design, dead matter produced life, mindlessness produced minds, and blind accident produced eyes. Their faith ignores all evidence to the contrary. Their commitment is absolute.

Atheist scientist Richard Lewontin freely admits that his rejection of a Creator is not based on evidence. It's where he starts. Before considering any facts or evidence, Lewontin rules out all "supernatural explanations of the world." He admits that scientists who deny God sometimes clash with common sense, but he still sides with their atheistic approach. Why? "Because we have a prior commitment, a commitment to materialism." By *materialism* he means the belief that "we exist as material beings in a material world, all of whose phenomena are the consequences of material relations among material entities." Even before we study any evidence, we must rule out God and make an up-front commitment to materialism. "That materialism is absolute," Lewinton explains, "for we cannot allow a Divine Foot in the door." Some schools and universities might give students the impression that if a scientific theory denies the Creator, the denial is based on evidence. But it's not based on evidence; it's based on a prior commitment to materialism and an absolute refusal to consider the Creator.

Atheist evolutionists can't deny that living things give a strong impression of design. Atheist Richard Dawkins says, "Biology is the study of things that give the appearance of having been designed for a purpose." Atheist George Gaylord Simpson says, "An eye, an ear, or a hand is a complex mechanism serving a particular function. It looks as if it had been made for a purpose. This appearance of purpose is pervading in nature." Atheist Francis Crick says, "The cell is thus a minute factory, bustling with rapid, organized chemical activity." These atheists don't claim, "Nothing looks as if it had been designed." They see many things that appear to be designed.

If you look at a watch, the sensible conclusion is that a watchmaker designed it. So when you see far more intricate designs in creation, what should you conclude? Richard Dawkins writes,

> All appearances to the contrary, the only watchmaker in nature is the blind forces of physics... Natural selection, the blind, unconscious automatic process ... which we now know is the explanation for the existence and apparently purposeful form of all life, has no purpose in mind.

Notice the wording. Dawkins says "all appearances to the contrary," so he admits that his faith in the blind forces of physics goes against what looks like obvious design. He speaks of the "apparently purposeful form of all life," thus admitting that his faith in a purposeless process goes against what seems apparent. He rejects purpose and design, not because he can't see it, but because he refuses to believe what he sees. His faith commitment to atheism matters more than observed evidence. Dawkins insists, "Even if there were no actual evidence in favor of the Darwinian theory, we should still be justified in preferring it over all rival theories." Regardless of whether the theory fits the facts, it fits his faith commitment to atheism.

Natural Causes?

Atheist scientists admit that cells, organs, and bodies operate as interconnected, complex systems and appear to be designed. But appearances are deceiving, they say, and what appears to be designed can all be explained as the result of random, undirected evolution. Not only *can* it be explained that way; it *must* be explained that way. No other explanation may even be considered. Intelligent design, they say, is an unscientific concept, unworthy to be researched by scientists or discussed in schools.

Picture a crime scene. A dead body is found with a knife in its chest. The knife is covered with the killer's fingerprints. The victim's hand is still grasping a clump of hair pulled from the head of the killer during a struggle. Investigators are told to gather the evidence and to explain what happened. But they are also ordered ahead of time to rule that this person died of natural causes. They are not permitted to investigate whether another person might have caused the death by some sudden action. Their only job is to explain how natural causes produced the death and the knife in the chest. They are not allowed to speak of homicide or to search for a killer. Even if they find someone whose fingerprints match those on the knife and whose DNA matches the hair in the victim's hand, the investigators are not allowed to explore whether this person killed the victim. The death must be explained by natural or accidental causes.

Those are the naturalistic, materialistic, atheistic ground rules for looking at the created world. God's fingerprints are all over the created world, and evidence of who created the universe is in our grasp as surely as hair in the hand of a crime victim. But any God-talk is declared "unscientific." No matter how exactly physical processes fit mathematical formulas, it is forbidden to speak of a Genius who designed matter in mathematical patterns and gave us minds to do math. No matter how much information is encoded in DNA, it is forbidden to speak of intelligence behind the information. No matter how ridiculous it is to say that something came from nothing, that life sprang from dead molecules, that mind emerged from mindless matter, this is the position of secular scientists and educators. The Creator must not be mentioned. Everything comes from natural causes.

Not everyone is willing to play by their rules, however. Scientists in the intelligent design movement look at DNA information or at a bacterial flagellum and see design. The intelligent design movement isn't revealing a secret unknown to ordinary people. It is merely stating the obvious, using more technical language and in-depth analysis. Any parent looking at a baby's face can see divine design. Any child looking at a starry sky can see divine design. Intelligent design scholars just explore deeper levels and use more careful reasoning to help scientists admit what is already obvious to almost everyone else: the universe, the earth, and living things appear to be products of divine design.

Looking at DNA, cells, and bodily organs and then crediting these things to random forces and gradual change is like looking at Mount Rushmore and crediting it to wind erosion rather than a sculptor. Mount Rushmore certainly looks like someone carved in stone the faces of presidents Washington, Jefferson, Roosevelt, and Lincoln. Are we to think that any resemblance of the rock to those presidents is accidental? Are we to think that any stories about a sculptor designing the faces on Mount Rushmore must be nothing but myth? No, say intelligent design thinkers, it's obvious that Mount Rushmore was designed and shaped with a purpose, and it's also obvious—even if we try to suppress the truth—that life was designed and shaped with a purpose.

The world is brimming with marvels that enchant little children and astound learned scientists. Underlying the almost magical qualities of various creatures are mechanical designs that display God's mind-boggling wisdom. Can anyone imagine the intelligence of the divine designer of DNA who packed such incredible amounts of information into such a small space? Can anyone fathom the power of the Lord who brought into being living creatures and vast galaxies without having any raw material to start with except his own boundless power? Can anyone grasp the artistic genius of the God who dreamed up all the different creatures with no prompting or pattern but his own creativity?

Mice and Music

God's creation displays something of his wisdom, power, and glory, but God himself remains invisible to us. This does not make him unreal. It just means that he is not part of his creation. God made all things, but he transcends the things he has made. Physical evidence points to God, but God himself is not physical. God is spirit, and we should not expect to find him as just one more item in the physical universe.

British author John Young told a parable about a community of mice. These mice lived in a place that opened into a music room with a grand piano. Sometimes, through the door of their home, they could hear beautiful music coming from the piano. They sighed in amazement at the beauty of the music. Soon, however, the mice got into a disagreement.

Some said, "There couldn't be music like that without a musician." But other mice said, "Nonsense. There is no musician." Still others were agnostics: "We'll never know whether there is a musician or not. Now get on with sharing the cheese."

One day, when the music began to play, a particularly bold and curious mouse decided to venture into the music room and see for himself. He scurried across the floor and scrambled up the shiny black leg of the grand piano. He peered into the piano for a few moments, and then hustled back home to the other mice, breathless with excitement at his discovery: "I have seen how music is made. I saw many tiny hammers striking tight wires. But I saw no musician."

The atheist mice nodded and smiled with satisfaction. The agnostics shrugged and continued eating their cheese. Those who had believed in a musician were disappointed. At least they knew the truth now, but life seemed a lot less interesting.

The mice think their question has been answered. They know a bit more about hammers and wires, and they think they know everything. They know something of the way a piano makes music, and they think they've proved that nobody designed the piano and that the piano can play itself. Of course there's no designer or musician inside the piano, but does that mean he doesn't exist? No, it just means that the musician is not part of the piano.

When we look at creation, we don't see the Creator, but does that mean he doesn't exist? No, it just means he's not part of his creation. We don't see him, but the designs of creation are clear evidence of a Designer, and the music of creation is clear evidence of a Musician. If it takes great mechanical skill to make a piano and if it takes great artistry to play a piano well, then what shall we say of God's mechanical skill in designing the intricate structures of the universe and his artistry in making his universe sing with such splendor?

Chapter 2

Personal Evidence of the Creator

Physical evidence of the Creator is all around you, and within you is personal evidence of the Creator. Implanted in you are capacities of the human spirit: thought, conscience, choice, love, and longing, to name a few.

Denying the Creator means denying all these. If you are the accidental result of a purposeless process, human personhood is not real. Your mind, your conscience, your will, your love, and your longings are illusions. They are byproducts of biochemistry. In his book *The Astonishing Hypothesis*, Francis Crick writes,

The Astonishing Hypothesis is that 'You,' your joys and sorrows, your memories and your ambitions, your sense of personal identity and free will, are in fact no more than the behavior of a vast assembly of nerve cells and their associated molecules.

Phillip Johnson points out that we might not take Crick seriously if he just came out and said, "I, Francis Crick, my opinions and my science, and even the thoughts expressed in this book consist of nothing more than the behavior of a vast assembly of nerve cells and their associated molecules." Crick's hypothesis is self-refuting. If he has no personal identity, why listen to him? If his thoughts are nothing but nerves and molecules interacting, why pay any attention to them?

Humanity is not the result of a purposeless process. We are created by God. In fact, God's original purpose in creating humans was to picture something of what God himself is like. "God created humanity in his own image" (Genesis 1:27). As God's image bearers, we humans are more like God than anything else in our world, so our capacities as persons are even stronger evidence for God's reality than the design and splendor of the world around us.

Thought

Consider the reality of human thought. You have the ability to think, remember, make deductions, use language, and communicate with others. But how do you know that your thoughts have anything to do with reality? How do you know that anything exists outside your own mind? How do you know it's not all an illusion? How do you know other people exist? How do you know it's not all a dream? You can't prove it. And yet you can't help believing it. You just know it. Or how about memory? How do you know you didn't pop into existence five minutes ago with a brain full of signals that merely seem like memories? You can't prove your memories are real—you just know it. And why? It's part of the way God made you.

Only because of the Creator can we have any confidence in the human mind. If you accept the notion that all human thoughts are nothing but impulses in a randomly evolved blob of meat (the brain), you have no basis for confidence that you have any capacity for knowing truth. Charles Darwin once asked, "Would anyone trust the convictions of a monkey's mind?" Darwin sensed that his theory of undirected evolution destroyed confidence in human thinking.

There's a great irony here. Atheistic evolutionists insist that their view is far more rational than believing in a Creator—but it turns out that if you see humanity as the result of a random process, you destroy human rationality. You have no ground for supposing that human thoughts—including your own—have any link to reality. William Provine once said that in order to believe in God, you have to drop off your brain at the churchhouse door. But who is dropping off his brain? Provine's atheism says that his own brain is an accident and that all his beliefs are accidental. How can he be so sure he knows the history of the universe and the origin of man? How can he claim to *know* anything at all? Why should he suppose that the accidental ideas in his accidental brain are in touch with reality?

If you deny the Creator and claim that your mind is just a jumble of chemical reactions that are the accidental outcome of a mindless process, what basis do you have for supposing that your mind is in touch with reality or that your train of thought is valid? None at all. But if you believe that a supreme Intelligence made the world intelligible and made your mind intelligent (to some degree, at least), then you have a basis for thinking your mind really can know something about the world around you. You don't have the infinite mind and unlimited knowledge of God, but your Creator has given you mental capacities and language skills to connect you with truth.

Conscience and Choice

Inside you is another pointer to God's reality: conscience. Your conscience senses a moral law outside you that you are either keeping or violating. But if there is no Creator of conscience and no Lawgiver, your sense of right and wrong has no basis in reality. If the conscience is really nothing but random chemistry in a random brain, why pay attention to it? If there's no Creator, why suppose there's any supreme standard of right and wrong? Without a Creator, you don't really have a conscience, and there is no moral standard for your conscience to recognize.

If choice is totally determined by physical processes and the forces of evolution, then there is no such thing as choice. In that case, as Charles Darwin put it, "wickedness is no more a man's fault than bodily disease!" In the words of William Provine, "there are no inherent moral or ethical laws, no absolute guiding principles for human society."

Atheist evolutionist Richard Rorty insisted that humans are not designed to know what is true or to seek what is right: "The idea that one species of organism is, unlike all the others, oriented not just toward its own increased prosperity but toward Truth, is as un-Darwinian as the idea that every human being has a built-in moral compass—a conscience." Therefore, insisted

Rorty, we must give up on truth and morality. But if atheistic Darwinism has no room for truth and morality, why give up on truth and morality? Why not give up on atheistic Darwinism instead?

The Creator is real. Because he designed us to resemble him, God's character is the original pattern for our character. We're created to image God's goodness and love. This is the basis of moral standards. We somehow know that not all behavior is equally right. Each of us has a conscience, a God-given internal sensor of whether we are matching the standard set by God. Our conscience has been damaged by sin and influenced by social forces, so we don't always agree on the exact details of what's right or wrong, but we know there is a higher standard, even when we disagree about some details. The very fact that we argue with others about what is right means that we're appealing to a standard higher than ourselves. Our awareness of a higher standard and the tug of our conscience point us to the reality of our Creator.

Relationships and Love

Another pointer to the reality of God is our capacity for relationships. We flourish best when we love and are being loved. Without love, life is hardly worth living.

Atheistic evolutionism reduces all relationships to mere biology and the drive to survive. In the words of Richard Dawkins, "We are survival machines—robot vehicles blindly programmed to preserve the selfish molecules known as genes." (Here's yet another reference to machines and programming from someone who denies design.) In this view, romance and long-term commitment and friendship are really nothing but molecular reactions.

Family bonds are just evolutionary adaptations to insure the propagation of one's own genes. Even behavior that seems completely unselfish can be explained in evolutionary terms. A soldier who falls on a grenade to save his companions, a doctor who leaves a lucrative practice to work in a desperately poor neighborhood for little pay—there's got to be some evolutionary instinct that can explain it. These explanations are often so farfetched they're comical, and yet they're presented with a straight face and the claim that now you know the real, *rational* explanations.

If you want to understand people and their relationships, you need to consider more than just biology or chemistry or physics. Romance and marriage involve a spiritual chemistry that's more than just body chemicals. Friendship and loyalty have a deeper basis than just the survival of DNA similar to one's own. Promises have a meaning rooted not just in survival instincts but in the faithfulness of God. Our experience of love in human relationships points us to the God of love who created us.

Longing and Hope

Within each of us is a longing for unlimited life and happiness. Nothing less can satisfy us. We crave joy without measure and life without end. We crave God. This craving is evidence of God's reality.

Some people argue the opposite. They grant that most people seem to have spiritual longings, but they use this fact to argue that God is not real, that he is just wishful thinking. Psychologist Sigmund Freud rejected belief in God and pictured religion as a crutch for emotionally needy people. According to Freud, people are afraid of the wild world around them and the wild urges within them. They yearn for a father-figure to protect them from dangers and to direct their urges in proper channels. This longing is so strong that it moves people to believe in God, without evidence or reasoning. They are moved by primitive longing, not rational thinking.

Freud was on to something when he pointed out the power of wishful thinking. People sometimes make themselves believe what they want to believe. But isn't this also true of those who don't believe in God?

Many people find it more convenient to be atheists than to believe in a God who might limit them or disapprove of their behavior. Aldous Huxley, author of *Brave New World*, admitted that his unbelief was not just a rational result of scientific research or logical reasoning. He said that he and many of his fellow atheists *wanted* the world to have no God and no moral standard. "We objected to the morality," said Huxley, "because it interfered with our sexual freedom." Huxley's atheism was wishful thinking.

Atheist philosopher Friedrich Nietzsche said, "If there were gods, how could I bear not to be a god? *Hence* there are no gods." Nietzsche didn't use evidence or reasoning to prove that there is no God or supernatural reality. He was so eager for his own will to be supreme that he found God's reality unbearable. Nietzsche's atheism was wishful thinking.

So if you dismiss belief in God as wishful thinking, keep in mind that not believing in God can also be wishful thinking. And if you agree with Freud that religion is really just a yearning for a father-figure, don't overlook the fact that many atheists (including Freud himself) had serious problems relating to their fathers. Their rejection of God may have been their way of rejecting any sort of father-figure.

The psychological argument against God says that belief in God comes not from rational thought but from a deep, non-rational urge. Even if that were true, the question remains: why do so many humans have this urge? Why, in almost every human culture, is there an urge to believe in Someone higher than ourselves? Atheism seldom comes naturally; you must talk yourself into it. Skeptics try to explain God away and claim that the deep urge to believe in God is an irrational instinct and a sign that God is a human invention, not a divine reality. But what would you expect if God is real and made humans for fellowship with him? Wouldn't you expect people to have powerful longings that often go deeper than rational analysis and explanation?

Almost all babies are born with a sucking instinct. They have this instinct without doing any logical reasoning about the existence of mothers. Would anyone claim mothers are not real because babies have an urge to suck that isn't based on logic? Of course not. The sucking instinct is a sign that babies come from mothers and are designed to thrive on mother's milk. So why claim that God isn't real because people have an urge to believe that isn't based on logic but on a deep, basic longing? What if this longing is a sign that humans come from God and are designed to thrive on fellowship with him?

The Bible never pretends that believers in God follow logic alone without any deep cravings. Rather, biblical writers say, "My heart and my flesh cry out for the living God" (Psalm 84:2). "As the deer pants for streams of water, so my soul pants for you, O God. My soul thirsts for God, for the living God" (Psalm 42:1-2). The Lord is a living reality, not just a philosophical proof or a mathematical formula, so a craving for God is a strong sign that he is there, not a proof that he isn't. Saint Augustine once wrote, "Lord, you have made us for yourself, and our hearts are restless until they rest in you." Even agnostics and atheists wonder about God sometimes and feel an urge to believe in him, though they continue to suppress this urge. The craving for God arises at some point in almost everybody.

A skeptic might point out that a craving doesn't prove that what you crave is real. If you're stranded in the desert, you might have a burning thirst for water, but that doesn't mean water is there for you. You might see a mirage in the distance and think it's water, but that doesn't make the water real. Likewise, you might want God and imagine God is out there, yet be mistaken.

Craving something doesn't prove you'll get it. Fair enough. But the craving still might reveal something about reality. It would be strange to crave water if no such thing as water existed anywhere. Stephen Evans writes,

> The fact that people in general have a need for water is strong evidence that there is such a thing as water, though this does not imply that an individual person will get water on a specific occasion. In a similar manner, the fact that we have a deep need to believe in and find God strongly suggests that God is real, though of course this does not mean that any one of us will actually discover

God and establish a relationship with him. It would be very odd indeed if we had a fundamental need for something that did not exist.

Most people seem to have a built-in craving for a higher, supernatural reality. If this craving were our only indicator of God, we might dismiss it as wishful thinking. But there is so much other evidence of the Creator: evidence in the design and splendor we see around us, and evidence in the capacities we find within us. The Creator is real, and he has made us for himself. Each of us has a hole in the soul that only God can fill, a craving that only God can satisfy. God has put eternity in the human heart (Ecclesiastes 3:11). We have a yearning for everlasting life. We have a need to know the infinite God.

Atheistic materialism cannot explain this craving for God and eternity, and it certainly cannot satisfy it. Instead, it can only offer despair and death. Atheist Bertrand Russell declared,

> Man is the product of causes which had no prevision of the end they were achieving; his origin, his growth, his hopes and fears, his loves and his beliefs, are only the outcome of accidental clusters of atoms and molecules; no fire, no heroism, no intensity of thought and feeling, can preserve an individual life beyond the grave; all the labors of the ages, all the devotion, all the inspiration, all the noonday brightness of human genius, are destined to extinction in the vast death of the solar system; the whole temple of man's achievements must inevitably be buried beneath the debris of a universe in ruins—all these things, if not quite beyond dispute, are yet so nearly certain that no philosophy which rejects them can hope to stand.... Only on the firm foundation of unyielding despair, can the soul's habitation henceforth be built.

That last sentence says it all: atheistic evolution offers unyielding despair. Life has no meaning and no lasting hope. As Russell put it, "There is darkness without, and when I die there will be darkness within. There is no splendor, no vastness anywhere, only triviality for a moment, and then nothing." Other atheists have likewise emphasized that the universe is indifferent to us and that we have no eternal future.

Are You Really You?

Denying the Creator—whether as a materialist who believes only in matter and molecules, or as a Buddhist who accepts the doctrine of no self—leaves us without any basis for supposing that human thought, conscience, choice, relationships, and longing have any meaningful reality. Your thinking isn't really thought, your feelings aren't really feelings, and your will isn't really making any choices. In fact, you're not really you. You may think you're a person with an individual consciousness, but you're not. According to atheistic materialism, you're just a complex machine that's arisen after a long series of chemical accidents. Everything about you is just a chemical accident. Language is a chemical accident. Memory is a chemical accident. Reasoning is a chemical accident. Conscience is a chemical accident. Choice is a chemical accident. Love is a chemical accident. Courage is a chemical accident. The longing for God and immortality is a chemical accident.

What sense does it make to believe this? It contradicts everything you know about yourself. You are you. You know that the human spirit, with its many capacities, is as real as the human body. Atheistic materialism denies the design of the body and the reality of spirit. A sound theory is supposed to explain known facts, and atheistic materialism can't explain things like thought, conscience, choice, love, longing, and other aspects of human personhood. It just tries to explain them away.

But come on! We know these things are real. They are essential to our humanity. We know we're not just machines (though our bodies are designed more marvelously than any machine ever built). When we recognize the marvels of our bodily design and pay attention to the personal capacities of the human spirit, we see strong evidence of a personal Creator.

Around us and within us are clues of a Creator. "Since the creation of the world God's invisible qualities—his eternal power and divine nature—have been clearly seen, being understood from what has been made" (Romans 1:20). "The heavens declare the glory of God; the skies proclaim the work of his hands" (Psalm 19:1). "The whole earth is full of his glory" (Isaiah 6:3). "How many are your works, O Lord! In wisdom you made them all" (Psalm 104:24). "I praise you because I am fearfully and wonderfully made; your works are wonderful" (Psalm 139:14). The Bible says these things, but you don't need the Bible to know them. The creation itself speaks volumes.

Chapter 3

Evaluating Evolution

Believing that God created all things doesn't rule out every form of evolution, especially if by evolution we simply mean changes within a group of living things over time. For example, the average size of finch beaks on a particular island varies from year to year as the environment changes. Nobody denies that this kind of adaptive change takes place. Nobody denies that animal breeders can develop different breeds of cattle and dogs by selecting for certain traits. Nobody denies that the different races of humanity trace back to the same ancestry and developed some different characteristics over time, such as different skin color and facial features. If that were all evolution meant, there would be no argument.

But often *evolution* is used not just as a word for changes within a population but as a word for a grand scheme which explains the origin of every form of life apart from God. Alvin Plantinga points out five main claims of this grand evolutionary scheme: First, the universe is very ancient, perhaps even billions of years old. Second, over time life has progressed from relatively simple forms of life to relatively complex forms of life, and eventually there were fish, then reptiles, then birds, then mammals, and finally, human beings. Third, all of these life forms have common ancestry; life originated at only one place on earth, and all living things today are descended from those original life forms. Fourth, this development over the generations is due to entirely natural processes, such as random genetic mutation and survival of the fittest. Fifth, life itself originally developed from non-living matter just by virtue of the ordinary laws of physics and chemistry, without any creative activity of God. All five claims, taken together, form the grand evolutionary picture.

These are different claims. They don't necessarily go together. There are people who accept all these claims; there are people who reject all of them; but there are also people who believe some of these claims but not others. For example, some folks think the universe is old and may even think that all living things share common ancestry, but they don't believe this happened randomly or apart from God's creative activity. The different claims can be distinguished from one another, so it may be helpful to consider them separately.

Did Chance Produce All Forms of Life?

Let's do this in reverse order and begin with the last two ideas, that the development of life from one form to another happened by chance, and that the original forms of life emerged from non-living matter by chance, apart from any divine design or action. These are the claims that are most obviously in conflict with biblical teaching about creation—and these are also claims for which there is not a shred of scientific evidence.

The notion that life emerged from non-living chemicals by chance, through purely naturalistic means, is wildly unlikely. Our smartest scientists have tried over and over to produce life from lifeless material and have failed, so it's extremely improbable that such a thing could happen by accident. Darwin himself thought this claim was iffy, and recent discoveries in molecular biology make it far less plausible than it was in Darwin's day. Back then scientists thought cells were fairly simple things. But we now know that even the simplest living cells are irreducibly complex and precisely coordinated. Even the simplest cell can't live unless all the complex interactions are working from the start. There's no scientific evidence to exclude a higher intelligence as the designer and creator of the first life forms; on the contrary, there's clear evidence of intelligent design.

Likewise, there's no evidence for the idea that various forms of plant and animal life evolved by purely natural processes. Even if there were a process of evolution from one life form to another—and that's not at all certain—there would still be no proof whatsoever that God did not direct the process. It is very hard to see how delicate instruments like the eye and the ear, which involve many complex parts working in coordination with each other, could develop by pure accident. Any claim that such developments could occur by chance is without evidence.

In his book *Evolution and the Myth of Creationism*, Tim Berra compares the evolution of animals to the evolution of cars. He describes how the splendid Corvette "evolved from more mundane automotive ancestors in 1953." He tells of the various steps and changes in later models which have led up to the present model of the Corvette. "A similar process," writes Berra, "shapes the evolution of organisms." Berra says the "evolution" of the Corvette illustrates the way natural forces randomly produce a changing sequence of organisms. But every Corvette in the sequence was designed by engineers! Those Corvettes didn't result from one car giving birth to another that was similar in some ways and different in others. The similarities and differences were designed by the cars' creators, as Phillip Johnson points out. Berra's example doesn't support blind evolution at all. It shows that intelligent designers can build something, and then, in later models, they can add variations to their basic plan.

Richard Dawkins makes a similar mistake. He says that a fast computer generating thousands of random letters of the alphabet per second would eventually produce any book you want, as long as the computer knew what text it wanted ahead of time and saved the randomly generated letters whenever they matched the desired result. This supposedly shows that random mutation and natural selection could produce the genetic codes for all the various life forms, apart from divine design. But how does a comparison to computers disprove intelligent design? Every computer and every program is a product of high intelligence, not a chance occurrence.

Atheists, in their effort to show that everything develops by chance and not by intelligent design, keep comparing various forms of life to machines. They describe evolution as a mechanistic process. But every machine or mechanistic process we're familiar with is the result of intelligent design.

There are no scientific grounds for denying that life was originally created by a great life-giver and that every later life form was designed by a higher intelligence. The claim that God did not design and make the various forms of life is based on a narrow-minded commitment to atheism, not on what seems most probable in light of evidence and logical reasoning. The clearest and most important aspect of the biblical story of creation is that God did it; and when the grand evolutionary scheme denies God's involvement, it is all bluff and no evidence.

Common Ancestry or Common Design?

What about the second and third claims in the grand scheme of evolution, that simpler life forms appeared before more complex life forms, and that all these forms of life are related through common ancestry? Well, when it comes to the sequence, there's not much argument. The Bible says plants came first, then fish and birds, then land animals and people. Almost every scientist would pretty much agree with that basic sequence.

But what's the explanation for that sequence? Darwin and his disciples see it as an indication that all living things trace back to a common ancestor and gradually evolved and became more complex over time. But what if similarities in structure and successive developments point not to the same ancestry but to the same Creator? Things which Darwinists see as proof of common ancestry can just as easily be seen as proof of common design.

Some people believe both common design *and* common ancestry. They believe that God created all things and that he designed the process of evolution from one life form to another as his way of accomplishing this. No doubt God could have done it that way if he chose, but the scientific evidence for this is spotty.

Charles Darwin predicted that if his theory of common ancestry was true, fossil hunters would eventually find huge numbers of transitional forms of life between the major groups. That hasn't happened. Harvard scientist Stephen Jay Gould complained about "the extreme rarity of transitional forms in the fossil record." Darwin also predicted that animal breeders would use the power of selection to produce radically new kinds of animals. That hasn't happened either. Selective breeding can produce variety within a life form, but it hasn't produced new forms.

Genesis says that God created each living thing after its kind. God could have done this through an evolutionary process if he wished, but the most straightforward reading of Scripture seems to indicate that God created each of the main families of life as separate and special (with room for development and adaptation within each family). There's little scientific data to contradict this or to support a theory of gradual development of all life from the same ancestor. Common ancestry appeals to some people not because the evidence demands it but because they are uneasy with anything sudden or miraculous and prefer something gradual and natural.

Young Earth or Old Earth?

There's one more claim of Darwinism that we haven't evaluated yet: the claim that the world is billions of years old. The evidence and arguments for this may be stronger than for some of the other claims. Notice, though, that this claim can be separated from the other claims. Even if the earth is very old, it doesn't prove common ancestry, and it certainly doesn't disprove the Creator.

Different Christians have different opinions about the earth's age. Some Christians think the Bible teaches a relatively young earth and aren't convinced by theories that the universe is extremely old. Perhaps there are flaws in the methods which scientists use to estimate the earth's age. After all, when people take the results of a few hundred years of study and try to project it over millions and even billions of years, it's possible their estimates will turn out to be badly mistaken. Rocks don't come with a date written on them. Light doesn't arrive from distant stars with a clock showing how long it took. Dating methods involve many assumptions and long chains of inference. At present, a particular dating method may seem to support an ancient earth, but in the future, science may change its mind in response to new data or revised assumptions.

Other Christians, though, are persuaded that astronomy, geology, and paleontology all point to a very old earth. They take the scientific evidence for an old earth to be very strong, and that's just fine with them, because it's consistent with the way they understand Genesis. They take the early chapters of Genesis as God's easy-to-understand way of saying he created and rules all things. God put this in the form of a story that used nontechnical, simple, sometimes figurative language so that anyone hearing the story could get the main point.

Suppose you had a little child who asked you, "Where do babies come from?" You might not give the child the kind of answer you would give a biology professor testing you on the processes of conception and fetal development. You might tell the child that babies come from the love of Mommy and Daddy, and you might give simplified descriptions of body parts and use a few figures of speech. The explanation you give a child might leave out some details and technical terms that you would include on the biology test. You're not trying to give the child an exact scientific explanation. Does that mean it's a poorer explanation? Not necessarily. In fact, it might be richer in some ways. When telling a child of the love between Daddy and Mommy, you would be saying something deeper than any technical details on a biology exam. Of course, in giving a child a simplified description with some figures of speech, you should still tell the basic truth, even if you're not trying to impress a biology professor. Mommy and Daddy are real, not just figurative. If you give the child basic information about body parts, the information should be true, not false, even if you use everyday language and maybe a few figures of speech. You would not help a curious child at all if you said, "The stork brings babies." That's just a tall tale.

When we ask, "Where did the world and living things and people come from," the early chapters of Genesis do not offer detailed scientific descriptions, but neither do they offer a stork-like tall tale. They offer simplified history for people of all ages. When we dig into details, we might not always know for sure whether this or that detail of the story is literal or figurative, but the main facts are clear: God created the universe; the first humans fell into sin after being tempted by an evil power; and this has affected all of humanity and everything on earth. Genesis does not offer all the answers that a scientist seeks to learn, but it's not just a tall tale. It is a true story that has communicated the greatest, deepest truths about creation to countless cultures throughout the ages.

Some Christians are convinced the earth is billions of years old and don't think creation occurred in six 24-hour days. They don't think science supports this view, and they don't think the Bible teaches it. Other Christians believe the Bible teaches creation in six ordinary days and are not persuaded by scientific claims about billions of years. All Christians agree that God is the Creator, but they differ on the best way to unite a sound understanding of the Bible with sound science. For myself, if I must err in studying the creation account in Genesis, I prefer to err on the side of taking it too literally. But if I must err in dealing with Christians who don't agree with my view, I want to err on the side of treating them too kindly. Old-earth creationists should not regard young-earth creationists as scientifically illiterate, and young-earth creationists should not regard old-earth creationists as spiritually bankrupt.

First Things First

The central truth of the creation story is that God did it. That's not the only thing Genesis says, but it's the most important thing. It's also the most obvious thing when we look at the world around us and at the capacities within us: there must be a Creator! If you're not sure how to square science with the Bible, don't get hung up on secondary questions. If you wonder whether God created all things, don't start by asking about the earth's age, and don't start by asking about common ancestry. First things first: start by asking whether a random process could produce the amazing design and the wondrous splendor that are evident in the world around you, as well as the special capacities of the human spirit within you. Don't let your uncertainty about lesser things keep you from believing the first and most obvious thing: the Creator is real.

Chapter 4

Sweet Signals

It's a gorgeous summer day, and you're relaxing on a sunny beach. Your skin soaks up the rays. You lie there without a worry in the world. A bead of sweat trickles down the side of your face. You start to feel a bit overheated, so you hop up and plunge into the water. The refreshing coolness washes over your hot skin. What a feeling! You spend a few minutes in the water. Then you get out and relax in the sun again.

After a while, you again feel a little too hot. This time you deal with it by getting a monster ice cream cone. The ice cream is melting and dripping faster than you can lick it, but you do your best to keep up. Every lick of that delicious coolness tastes better than the last. As you swallow the last of it, you feel incredibly happy and content.

You've just had a religious experience.

What? How can that be? Soaking up the sun and splashing in the water and licking an ice cream cone—how can these things be religious experiences? What does ice cream have to do with God? Well, according to the Bible, it's got everything to do with God. Ice cream is a religious experience, a sweet signal from God.

For a lot of us, summer is a great time of year. Everything seems a little more lively and cheerful. We're outside more. We enjoy the fresh air. We talk with neighbors we don't see much in the winter. Children are playing and running and biking and rollerblading. The aroma of neighborhood grills is in the air.

Summer is a good time to get away from work for a while and do something special with friends or family. You can go water skiing, or fishing, or swimming, or rafting. You can roar along on your motorcycle and feel the breeze in your face. And to top it all off, summer is that wonderful, messy time for dribbling watermelon juice down your chin or smearing ice cream on your nose. All of these summertime pleasures are sweet signals from God. They are religious experiences.

If you're a churchgoer, it might sound sacrilegious to say that ice cream can be a religious experience. If you're not a churchgoer, it might sound silly. Good food and good times, a religious experience?

But it's not just my own idea to talk about food and fun this way. It's God's. We all have times when we feel great, when life seems good, when our hearts are full of joy. Those times don't come our way by chance. They are sweet signals from God. They are religious experiences. "The living God who made heaven and earth and sea and everything in them... has not left himself without testimony: He has shown kindness by giving you rain from heaven and crops in their seasons; he provides you with plenty of food and fills your hearts with joy" (Acts 14:15,17). In other words, every refreshing rainfall, every crop and garden, every hearty meal, all good things that fill your heart with happiness—including ice cream—are sweet signals from God himself, displays of his character, proofs of his kindness and care, and invitations to know him better.

Inventor of Happiness

Creation shows us a lot about the Lord who made it. In the first place, it shows that God is real. If the universe isn't everlasting—and only a tiny minority of scientists claim that it is—then it had to get started somehow, and something doesn't come from nothing. Somebody had to bring it into being.

And creation doesn't just show that God is real. It also shows that God is powerful, wise, and splendid. When you gaze up at the sky and think of the countless billions of stars and the vast reaches of space, when you stand before a mighty mountain or a roaring waterfall or a towering tree, you're overwhelmed by a sense of sheer greatness. When you study the patterns of nature, whether it's the intricacy of a flower or the order of a colony of ants, whether it's the unique crystal of each snowflake or the trademark swirls of each unduplicated fingerprint, you can only marvel at the astounding genius that lies behind it all. Who but Someone of unimaginable power, wisdom, and splendor could bring such things into being?

So then, creation testifies to God's reality, his splendor, his power, and his wisdom. But that's not all. Creation also testifies to God's joyfulness and his eagerness to fill our lives with joy. As we recognize the designs in creation as evidence of a Supreme Designer, we should also recognize fun and satisfaction as evidence of a Supreme Fun-Lover.

According to the Bible, God testifies to people, even to many who know little or nothing about him, by filling their stomachs with food and their hearts with joy. Why does the sun feel so good? Why does that ice cream taste so good? Why does that hamburger on the grill smell so good? Why does that lake or mountain look so splendid? Why do birds and brooks make such beautiful music? All these things are signals from a God who isn't just a genius or an architect or an efficiency expert. He's a great lover of joy, and his joy spills over into an outpouring of delight and fun for his creatures.

Why is the attraction between boys and girls so powerful and exciting? How can a husband and wife feel such overwhelming love and contentment just sitting next to each other looking out the window? And what about sexual intimacy? Who came up with the idea for that? Who dreamed up something so strange and yet so full of pleasure? Once again, it's God's idea. The Bible says, "May you rejoice in the wife of your youth. May her breasts satisfy you always, may you ever be captivated by her love" (Proverbs 5:18-19).

There's also the joy of children and grandchildren. Why do we have families? Why do we get that feeling of joy and awe when we hold a newborn baby? Why do we feel so excited when we see Mom's nose and Dad's brown eyes in that little face? Why do we smile proudly when our little one smiles at us, or starts to walk, or babbles a few words, or hits a home run, or graduates, or gets a worthwhile job? It's all God's doing. The joys of home and family come from God (Psalm 127:2, Psalm 113:9).

God gives other forms of enjoyment as well. Who gives a student or scholar or researcher the thrill of discovery? Who gives you that feeling of achievement after you've worked all day and you feel like you really got something done? Once again, it's a gift from God himself. "A man can do nothing better than to eat and drink and find satisfaction in his work. This too, I see, is from the hand of God, for without him, who can eat or find enjoyment?" (Ecclesiastes 2:24-25)

Food, fun, falling in love, enjoying family, feeling a sense of accomplishment—all these pleasures are sweet signals from the Lord about what kind of God he is. "The Lord is good to all... and loving toward all he has made... He gives them their food at the proper time... He satisfies the desires of every living thing... The Lord is faithful in all he does" (Psalm 145:9-16).

A Religious Response

Even if you never step into a church, even if you never open a Bible, even if you don't believe in God at all, you are having religious experiences all the time. God is continually sending signals and dropping hints and giving you a taste of his kindness and goodness. And here's something else you might not realize. When you have all these religious experiences, you're bound to have a religious response. Even if you don't consider yourself religious, you cannot help but have some sort of religious response to God's sweet signals. You cannot help but worship something and seek it as your highest good.

Your religion might be to worship happiness itself, instead of worshipping the God who gives you happiness.

Maybe your greatest happiness is physical pleasure. You live for food and sex and excitement. Let the good times roll! Eat, drink, and be merry! To you, pleasure isn't a gift from God. Pleasure *is* God. The Bible speaks of people "whose god is their stomach" (Philippians 3:19), who are "lovers of pleasure rather than lovers of God" (2 Timothy 3:4). But God didn't invent pleasure as a replacement for himself. He created it as a signal to draw us to him, as an appetizer to lead us to him and find our greatest pleasure in knowing him.

Or maybe your greatest happiness comes from friends or family. As long as you can be with buddies, or as long as your kids are thriving and making you proud, you're happy. You can't think of anything you want more. But God didn't give you these relationships as a replacement for himself. These relationships are a signal to attract you to the best relationship of all: friendship with God and a place in his family.

Or maybe you're happiest when you're working and getting that marvelous feeling of accomplishment and success. What satisfaction when your business succeeds, or when you get that promotion you've been wanting! If you're a workaholic, nothing matters more than feeling like you've done something important and moved up in the world. But God didn't make success as an end in itself. The satisfaction of work is just a taste of the joy we can experience when we work for God and do everything in partnership with our Creator.

God is constantly sending us signals, but we tend to misread the signals. We treat temporary hints of happiness as though they are the ultimate happiness, and we may even base entire religious systems on our misreading of the signals God sends.

In the past, when people wanted food and sex and pleasure more than anything else, they tended to invent gods and goddesses that symbolized these things. Some religions worshipped gods and goddesses of fertility. They put such an emphasis on finding happiness in created things that they ignored the Creator and worshiped idols who represented fun and fertility to them. Today there's a resurgence of nature worship and goddess worship. And among people who don't consider themselves religious, the basic principle of pleasure worship is powerful.

Other people come up with a different type of religion. They put less emphasis on pleasure, and they put an enormous emphasis on the family. They exalt the family so high that they're caught up in ancestor worship. They pray to the spirits of dead parents and grandparents and other ancestors. They also put such emphasis on producing children who see family as sacred that a child who doesn't meet the parents' expectations is a disgrace. Around the world, many people still today engage in ancestor worship. But even if you don't, you might still, in a more secular way, worship your family instead of worshiping the Lord who gives you your family.

Then there are the religions that take work and achievement as the ultimate. The satisfaction we feel at a job well done can be exalted and made the very basis for divine acceptance. Do this! Do that! Follow this road of meditation, or that path of good works, and you can move upward from one level to the next on the ladder of religious greatness, the way a good worker moves up the ladder of success. Many people embrace a religion of working their way up to God. But even if you don't have any religion of rituals or good deeds, you still might see achievement and excellence and self-reliance as the supreme values.

These are all ways of misreading the signals God sends us. We take God-given clues, and instead of seeing them as evidence pointing to Someone far greater, we idolize the things themselves. No wonder John Calvin described the human heart as a factory for idols!

Some people, seeing how foolish it is to worship things rather than God, have responded by taking a very different approach. They say that the physical world is an illusion, that all pleasure is evil, that everything earthly is bad, and that true religion means rejecting all these things and seeking God in a spiritual realm that has nothing to do with this present world. Perfection is found in refusing all the best-tasting foods and drinks, abstaining from marriage and sex and family, living as uncomfortably as possible, and learning to detach yourself from any kind of happiness in this life and learning to detach yourself from any particular ideas about God. True spirituality, in this approach, means total detachment, emptying the body of pleasures, emptying the mind of thoughts, and experiencing God as an impersonal void. However, that's a terrible error. If God created all these good things, if he's the one who fills our stomachs with food and our hearts with happiness, then it's insulting to God and cruel to people to say that God's good gifts are bad. Even though we often misuse some of those gifts, that doesn't mean the gifts themselves are bad. God's gifts are good (1 Timothy 4:4-5).

Seeking the Source

We shouldn't worship God's gifts and become obsessed with them, but we shouldn't despise those gifts either. They are part of God's testimony to us. They are sweet signals, clues of his kindness. And they are invitations to find our ultimate happiness in the Source of all happiness. The good things of creation are appetizers for an even better feast in God's new creation.

The signals God sends us can be very intense and beautiful and enjoyable. Even so, they are limited and temporary. Happiness isn't something we can grab for ourselves or hold within our grasp. It comes and then it goes. And yet these hints of happiness awaken a deep longing for a greater, more permanent happiness, an infinite, eternal happiness.

God has made everything beautiful in its time. He has also set eternity in the hearts of men; yet they cannot fathom what God has done from beginning to end. I know that there is nothing better for men than to be happy and do good while they live. That everyone may eat and drink and find satisfaction in all his toil—this is the gift of God. (Ecclesiastes 3:11-13).

Beauty, happiness, satisfaction—whether it's in a sunset or an ice cream cone or a family outing or a sense of achievement—these are gifts from a God who beckons us from the outside with hints of happiness, and who stirs us on the inside with a sense of eternity in our hearts. God has designed us in such a way that we will find his good gifts enjoyable and exciting and inviting but not, ultimately, fulfilling. "God did this so that men would seek him and perhaps reach out for him and find him ... 'For in him we live and move and have our being'" (Acts 17:27-28). God's purpose in sending sweet signals is that we will seek him, the Source of those signals.

When you experience intense happiness, you are having a religious experience, whether you realize it or not. And you will have a religious response, whether you intend to or not. You can't help it. You can react wrongly in various ways. But why not pursue another possibility? Why not seek God and "perhaps reach out for him and find him"? That's what God is signaling you to do.

Chapter 5

Supernatural Surprises

We find evidence of the Creator in the designs and wonders of the physical world, in the capacities of the human spirit, and in the sweet signals of good things we enjoy. Another way to know God's reality is through more direct contact with him.

Have you ever had a supernatural surprise, a close encounter with God when you didn't expect it? If so, you're not the only one. A great many people say they've had unexpected, overwhelming experiences of God's presence. I'm not talking about weird rumors or wild fantasies but about real people in real life situations: children, grownups, women, men, farmers, truckers, prison inmates, college students, newspaper writers, people of every sort. These experiences aren't limited to people with too much imagination and too little intelligence. Some very brilliant, rational people tell of supernatural surprises they've had.

Alvin Plantinga is one of the world's leading thinkers. He has taught philosophy at Yale, Harvard, Chicago, Calvin, and Notre Dame. His powers of logic are staggering. But for Dr. Plantinga, God isn't just an abstract idea for debate. God is a living reality.

Dr. Plantinga grew up in a Christian home and believed in the existence of God and in the truth of the Bible. As a young man, he left home and went off to Harvard University. He says,

I was struck by the enormous variety of spiritual and intellectual opinion at Harvard, and spent a great deal of time arguing about whether there was such a person as God... I began to wonder whether what I had always believed could really be true. At Harvard, there was such an enormous diversity of opinions about these matters, some of them held by highly intelligent and accomplished people who had little but contempt for what I believed.

But there on Harvard's campus, beset by doubts, far from home, surrounded by people who didn't believe in God as he did, something stunning happened. Alvin Plantinga writes:

> One gloomy evening I was returning from dinner. It was dark, windy, raining, nasty. But suddenly it was as if the heavens opened; I heard, so it seemed, music of overwhelming power and grandeur and sweetness; there was light of unimaginable splendor and beauty; it seemed I could see into heaven itself; and I suddenly saw or perhaps felt with great clarity and persuasion and conviction that the Lord was really there and was all I had thought. The effects of this experience lingered for a long time; I was still caught up in arguments about the existence of God, but they often seemed to me merely academic, of little existential concern.

If someone as brilliant and logical as Professor Plantinga could speak of such an experience and its long-term effect, then it's fair to say that supernatural surprises aren't just for weak-minded, illogical people. God is real, and God can come to anyone he wants anytime he wants in whatever way he wants. He may come when he's least expected. Alvin Plantinga found this out, and he wasn't the first.

The Lord is in This Place

The Bible tells of another young man, far from home, in a grim situation, feeling alone, who encountered God unexpectedly. This young man, Jacob, was a sneaky cheater. One day when Jacob's twin brother Esau was hungry, feeling absolutely famished, Jacob refused to give him food until Esau agreed to give his rightful inheritance to Jacob. Later, when their father Isaac was old and blind, Jacob came to his sightless father pretending to be Esau, and he stole the blessing his father intended for Esau. Esau was furious and started making plans to kill Jacob. So Jacob fled for his life.

When he reached a certain place, he stopped for the night because the sun had set. Taking one of the stones there, he put it under his head and lay down to sleep. He had a dream in which he saw a stairway resting on the earth, with its top reaching to heaven, and the angels of God were ascending and descending on it. There above it stood the Lord, and he said: "I am the Lord, the God of your father Abraham and the God of Isaac. I will give you and your descendants the land on which you are lying. Your descendants will be like the dust of the earth, and you will spread out to the west and to the east, to the north and to the south. All peoples on earth will be blessed through you and your offspring. I am with you and will watch over you wherever you go, and I will bring you back to this land. I will not leave you until I have done what I have promised you."

When Jacob awoke from his sleep, he thought, "Surely the Lord is in this place, and I was not aware of it." He was afraid and said, "How awesome is this place! This is none other than the house of God; this is the gate of heaven" (Genesis 28:11-17).

Have you ever had a supernatural surprise, an unexpected, overwhelming sense of God's reality? Have you ever thought, "Surely the Lord is in this place, and I was not aware of it"?

Many people encounter the Lord in powerful ways and in surprising places. For some people, this happens during the worst of times, maybe even when they come very near to death itself. They sense heaven connecting with earth in a way they never have before. More than one person has been able to say from an ambulance or an intensive care unit, "Surely the Lord was in this place, and I was not aware of it."

For others this happens at the best of times. A long-time atheist started to believe in God when his wife gave birth to their first baby. He held that baby in his arms, gazing at her, and his atheism collapsed. He was so amazed at the baby's marvelous design and so overwhelmed by love that he knew God was real and was right in that birthing room. God makes each baby in his image, so the birth of a new image-bearer can produce a powerful sense of God's presence. Again and again in delivery rooms and maternity wards, new parents whisper to themselves, "Surely the Lord is in this place, and I was not aware of it."

God's presence may be experienced almost anywhere. A prison inmate wrote in response to one of my radio programs:

> I was listening to the radio, and I was "flipping" between two rock-n-roll stations. I was going up the dial when my hand literally froze. There was a man preaching about Satan's power, and yet how Satan is still afraid of the gospel. I didn't know what to make of not being able to move the dial any further at that time. I listened to the program and prayed with the man. It was weird, praying with a radio, but I did anyhow! The stations then went into credits and weather, and all that time I was trying to figure out what had just taken place. Then it just hit me like a ton of bricks. I thought, "My God, I was just touched by the Holy Spirit." It was a remarkable feeling. I cried tears of joy. I'd heard stories but was always skeptical about them. Never again will I doubt the power of the Holy Spirit. Never again!

Even in prison, it can be said, "Surely the Lord is in this place, and I was not aware of it."

A Bizarre Bargain

Isn't it amazing how God so often finds us and connects with us right where we are? I met a trucker who told me the following story from his own life. He'd been ignoring God completely, and then one day he met one of his friends at a truck stop. His friend said, "What would happen if you smashed your truck and got killed? Would you go to heaven?" The trucker replied, "Hmmm. I don't know." His friend said, "Then you're in deep doo-doo, brother!" The trucker couldn't get his friend's question out of his mind. He thought, "What if God is real? What would he do with a guy like me?"

One day, he was driving down the road when he devised a bizarre bargain. The people who loaded his truck had overloaded it. It was carrying more than the legal weight limit, and he was worried. The first weigh station he came to, he would have to stop and have the load weighed. When they found his truck was too heavy, he'd have to pay a big fine and maybe even dump part of the load. That's when he decided to make a bargain. He said, "God, there's no way I'm going to drive hundreds of miles, past all those weigh stations, without at least one of them being open and catching me. But if none of the weigh stations are open, if I do make the whole trip without getting fined, I'll take that as a sign that you exist, God, and I'll start going to church beginning next Sunday."

As he continued driving, he saw not a single policeman. The first weigh station was closed ... and the next ... and the next. With every closed station the trucker passed, he felt greater relief and greater fear: relief that he wasn't getting caught, and fear that God had been listening to him. The further he drove, the tighter God's grip on him seemed to grow. He felt more and more overwhelmed with a sense that God was right there in that truck with him. When he finally made it to his destination, he had no choice. He went to church and took his wife along. Both of them ended up committing their lives to Christ. And they've never been the same since.

That bargain wasn't a very bright idea. It was not God's job to help that law-breaking trucker not to get caught. Later on, as the trucker got to know Jesus better and understood more about God and his ways, he realized how misguided and silly his bargain had been. He doesn't try to use God to get away with breaking the law anymore. But the fact remains that God took him up on his bargain, and the change in this trucker's life has been real. You just never know when you're going to get a supernatural surprise. Even in the cab of an eighteen-wheeler, knowing very little about God and making a bizarre bargain, a man can find himself saying, "Surely the Lord is in this place, and I was not aware of it."

Maybe you have your own story. Maybe you don't talk about it with others for fear of what they might say, but if you've ever had a supernatural surprise, you may still think of it as one of the most important things that's ever happened to you.

Thinking Things Through

What should we make of supernatural surprises? Is there something wrong with people who have them? Is there something wrong with people who *don't* have them? Let's think things through by going back to the story of Jacob.

Jacob was as shrewd as any professor, as crooked as any convict, and as eager to bargain as the most desperate truck driver. But he was also a man chosen by God. The Lord used the remarkable dream of a stairway between heaven and earth to get Jacob's attention. Jacob had heard about the Lord from his grandparents Abraham and Sarah, and from his parents Isaac and Rebekah; but now Jacob knew with absolute clarity that God was real and was addressing him personally.

God helped Jacob to see something that's true at every moment but is often hidden from us: there is a stairway, a connection between heaven and earth, by which God joins himself to his world and to his people. And on this stairway, God's angels are ascending and descending in constant activity. Angels are God's servants, working to accomplish his will; they are God's warriors, standing guard over his people; and they are God's messengers, bringing God's message to people who need it.

We don't usually see with our eyes the connection between heaven and earth, and we don't usually see the angels in visible form, but they are very real. Whether we realize it or not, we live each moment in the presence of the supernatural. One effect of a supernatural surprise is to impress this upon us as never before: "Surely the Lord is in this place, and I was not aware of it."

But the impression or experience isn't enough. We also need a Word from God. We need God's Word to help us understand his plan and purpose, and we need God's Word so that we'll have solid promises to live by even after the experience fades.

In Jacob's dream, the important thing wasn't just what God showed but what God said. God made it very clear to Jacob that the Lord wasn't some brand new God that no one had ever heard of before. God declared himself to be the God of Abraham and Isaac, and he declared to Jacob the very same plan and promises he'd spoken to those who'd gone before. God spoke of a promised land, of a chosen people who would continue to multiply, and of using this chosen people to bring blessing to the whole earth. This wasn't just a private revelation to inspire and comfort Jacob. It was a revelation of God's plan for history and for the whole world, and it was a gracious declaration that God had a place for Jacob in that plan.

Then the Lord got more personal with Jacob. He spoke four wonderful words: "I am with you." When those four words from God take root in your heart, you can handle any situation. "I am with you"—with those four words God promised Jacob his presence, and then he promised his protection. He said, "I am with you and will watch over you wherever you go." What a comfort to know that you're living under the protection of the Lord and of his mighty angels! And on top of his presence and protection, God promised Jacob a homecoming. He said, "I am with you and will watch over you wherever you go, and I will bring you back to this land. I will not leave you until I have done what I promised you." Jacob responded to all this by saying, "If God will be with me... then the Lord will be my God" (Genesis 28:20-21). Jacob took to heart what God promised, and Jacob promised to give himself to God.

God's words were even more important than the vision. Long after the vision faded, Jacob's mind rang with the message of a redemptive blessing that would reach down through history and all around the world. In all the ups and downs of his life, Jacob's mind echoed with God's promises of his presence, protection, and an eventual homecoming to a promised land.

Jacob lived very early in the unfolding of God's plan. Today you and I have the Word of God in all its fullness in the Bible. The Bible gives us truths that continue to uphold us long after the sensations of an experience have faded. We need the Word of God to provide our faith with staying power, and we also need God's Word to explain and evaluate our experiences.

If an experience leads you to contradict the God of the Bible and form your own pet notion of God, then you are mistaken. It may have been a demonic delusion, rather than a divine encounter. And even if it was a divine encounter, you've misunderstood it and twisted it and made an idol of it if you're ignoring what God says in his Word.

However, if the experience alerts you to the reality of the Lord, as it did with people I've mentioned, and if it opens your mind to God's plan of salvation described in the Bible, and if it opens your heart to receive personally his promises declared in the Bible, and if it gives you a deepening desire for fellowship with the Christ revealed in the Bible, then your experience is indeed a great blessing from God.

Stairway to Heaven

Let me share an experience of mine. I grew up in a Christian family, but as I was growing up, I began to ask hard questions. Does God exist? Is Jesus really alive? Do I belong to him? Or will he reject a boy who has so many sins and questions and doubts? If I can't be sure he's even there, how can I possibly be sure I belong to him? These questions filled me with dread.

One night I couldn't take it any more. I went to my mom and asked her what I should do. She told me, "Jesus says in the Bible that if you open the door and ask him to come in, he will come in and live with you. So just pray and ask him." And that's what I did. I got on my knees and talked to Jesus and asked him to be my Savior and to live in me.

My fears vanished. I went to bed and slept soundly. I woke up with a sense of warmth, joy, security and peace that I can't put into words. I think it was a taste of "the peace of God, which transcends all understanding" (Philippians 4:7).

Two nights later, I had a dream of heaven. I don't remember many details, but I recall a tremendous splendor and a sense of the presence of angels. To tell the truth, the particulars don't seem to matter much. More important was sheer delight that God is everything the Bible says he is, and that I am his child. My experience doesn't change anything the Bible says about God or heaven. It was God's way of confirming his love and his truth to a boy who trusted in Jesus. Since then, I've never had another dream like that one. But I believe by faith what God says in his Word, and I know I belong to Jesus.

What if you haven't had any astounding supernatural experiences? Does that mean something is wrong with you? Not necessarily. You don't need anything more dazzling than the good news of Jesus. The Spirit of God moves in many different ways. Not everybody needs the same experiences. But everybody needs the same Lord, the same Word of God, and the same Savior. Just believe God's Word, accept his promises in Christ, and trust that his Spirit is at work in you. That's what matters, not what experience led you to that point.

You and I need faith in Jesus, not faith in experiences. The stairway Jacob saw in his dream represents Jesus Christ himself. Jesus made this very clear when he told one of his friends, "I tell you the truth, you shall see heaven open, and the angels of God ascending and descending on the Son of Man" (John 1:51). Jesus was picturing himself as the stairway Jacob saw, with angels ascending and descending on it. Jesus is the stairway who connects heaven and earth, because he is a child of earth and at the same time the Lord of heaven. Jesus brings God to man, and man to God, because he is both God and man. Jesus is the ultimate meaning of Jacob's dream, and Jesus is the ultimate meaning of every genuine supernatural experience.

Chapter 6

The Person the Prophets Predicted

Atheism is hard to maintain. It rings hollow when it dismisses physical evidence of a Creator, explains away human personhood, and denies all supernatural experiences. Throughout history only a small minority of people have been atheists. The vast majority have believed in some kind of divine Being and have belonged to some sort of religion. But even if you reject atheism, how do you know what God is really like? How do you know which religion is true?

I am a Christian. But Christianity isn't the only religion around, the Bible isn't the only book around, and Jesus isn't the only leader to attract a following. So why be a Christian when you could be a Hindu or Muslim or Buddhist or something else instead? Why believe the Bible as the ultimate book when Muslims have the Koran, Hindus have the Bhagavad-Gita, and various others have their own book they consider sacred? Why trust Jesus as the supreme link between God and humanity, when so many people look to Muhammad or Confucius or the Buddha or someone else?

With many varieties of religion around, it may seem impossible to decide which is right. It's tempting just to say, "You believe whatever you want to believe, and I'll believe whatever I want to believe." That might help us to avoid conflict, but it won't bring us any closer to the truth. If we want our belief to be more than wishful thinking, then we can't just believe whatever we want to believe. We need to believe what's true.

I'll be blunt: If Christianity isn't true, then I don't want to be a Christian. If the Bible isn't God's Word, then I don't want to believe that it is. If Jesus isn't God come to us as a human, then I don't want to trust him or follow him.

On the other hand, if Christianity is true, then I'm not the only one who should be a Christian. You should be a Christian too. If the Bible is God's Word, then I'm not the only one who should believe it. You should believe it too. If Jesus is God with us and the Savior of the world, then I'm not the only one who should follow him. You should follow him too.

First, though, we need to settle the question whether there's anything that sets the Bible apart from other books and anything that sets Jesus apart from other religious leaders. Christians believe that the Bible is the Word of God written, totally reliable and without error in what it reveals. But *why* believe the Bible instead of another sacred book? Christians believe that Jesus is the Son of God and the Savior of all who trust him. But *why* believe in Jesus instead of some other religious leader?

Prophecies That Match a Person

There are a number of ways to approach this. We could explore archeology and manuscripts and various kinds of evidence that show the accuracy of the Bible. We could examine some historical and logical arguments that show it's rational to believe in Jesus. But instead of trying to make a case for the Bible, and then making a separate case for Jesus, let's focus on how Jesus and the Bible confirm each other. How do we know Jesus is the way? Because the Bible says so. And why should we believe what the Bible says? Because Jesus confirms it.

That may sound unhelpful and unconvincing at first. Isn't that just arguing in a circle? You might think, "The Bible and Jesus match up? Big deal! Of course the Christian holy book fits the founder of Christianity. The holy book of every religion records the ideas of its founder, so of course the man and the message match up. But what if the man and the book which matches him are both wrong?"

In the case of the Bible and Jesus, though, we're not just talking about a holy book that was written by a religious leader or by his followers as a record of what he taught. You see, the Bible isn't just one book; it's a collection of 66 books. 27 Bible books—those in the part called the New Testament—were written after Jesus walked this earth. These 27 New Testament books recorded what Jesus said and did. But the other 39 books in the Bible—those in the part called the Old Testament—were written *before* Jesus came. These 39 books, written centuries before Jesus, often spoke of events that still lay in the future. And here's the amazing thing. Those predictions came true, and they came true in the life of one particular person: Jesus!

Almost anybody can write a book, and almost any book can record things that have already happened and words that have already been spoken. But what about a book that pointed to events centuries before they happened? I think you'd agree that such a book would be amazing. I think you'd also agree that any person whose life fulfilled all sorts of ancient predictions—made in different writings from different centuries—would be an amazing person indeed. Jesus is such a person, and the Bible is such a book.

Predictions About Birth and Ministry

The books of the Old Testament contain many predictions about the birth of a future ruler and rescuer whom God would send to overcome evil and give people new life. These were not just vague predictions. Some details were quite specific. For example, the prophet Micah said that this ruler would be born in Bethlehem (5:2). The prophet Hosea said that God's Son would be called out of Egypt (11:1). The prophet Isaiah said that a virgin would become pregnant and give birth to a son (7:14). Isaiah also said that a great light would shine in the region of Galilee after the special child was born (9:1-2).

Now, it's a stunning prediction to say a virgin will give birth, and it sounds like an outright contradiction for different prophets to predict a child being born in Bethlehem, coming out of Egypt, and shining in Galilee. Bethlehem and Galilee are at opposite ends of Israel; Egypt is another country altogether. How could prophecies referring to Bethlehem, Egypt, and Galilee all be fulfilled in the same child? Sounds impossible, doesn't it?

Centuries later, a young woman from Nazareth in Galilee became pregnant without being with a man. This woman, Mary, was betrothed to Joseph. At first Joseph could not believe that Mary's pregnancy was a miracle, but an angel convinced him. The couple lived in Nazareth, so it seemed obvious that their baby would be born there, not in Bethlehem, far to the south. But then the Roman emperor called for a census and required people to register in the towns of their ancestry. Joseph and Mary had to go to Bethlehem, because Joseph's family line went back to King David, and Bethlehem was the city of David. While they were in Bethlehem for the census, Mary went into labor. Baby Jesus was born in Bethlehem, just as the prophet Micah predicted.

King Herod, the vicious ruler in that region, heard that a special baby had been born, and Herod felt threatened. He ordered the killing of all the baby boys in Bethlehem. Before the order could be carried out, however, an angel warned Joseph what Herod was planning. Joseph and Mary fled to Egypt with baby Jesus. Awhile later, King Herod died, and Jesus came up out of Egypt with Joseph and Mary, just as the prophet Hosea had predicted.

After leaving Egypt, the family went back to Israel, to the town of Nazareth in Galilee, where they originally came from. There Jesus grew up and began his ministry, bringing God's light to the region of Galilee, just as the prophet Isaiah predicted.

Amazing! The seemingly contradictory prophecies all came true in the Christ child: he was conceived of a virgin, born in Bethlehem, came out of Egypt, and was God's light in Galilee.

Through the prophet Isaiah, writing 700 years before Jesus' birth, God not only predicted that a baby would be born of a virgin and would be God with us (7:14), but the prophet also predicted that at the Messiah's coming, the eyes of the blind would be opened, the ears of the deaf would hear, and the lame would leap for joy (35:5-6). Even the most skeptical people who knew Jesus couldn't deny that he enabled blind people to see and deaf people to hear. Nobody could deny that Jesus made paralyzed people walk and leap and praise God. Even Jesus' worst enemies had to admit that he was doing amazing things. These miracles weren't just marvels to astonish people; they were signs that Jesus was the person the prophets predicted.

When Jesus' friend John the Baptizer was in prison, he sent a message to Jesus, asking, "Are you the one who was to come, or should we expect someone else?"

Jesus' answer was simple. He replied, "The blind receive sight, the lame walk, those who have leprosy are cured, the deaf hear, the dead are raised, and the good news is preached to the poor" (Matthew 11:3-5). These things showed that yes, Jesus was the promised Messiah, and no, the people shouldn't look elsewhere, because Jesus was doing the miracles that the Old Testament had predicted. Many of the common people, recalling those predictions and seeing Jesus in action, believed in him. They said, "When the Messiah comes, will he do more miraculous signs than this man?" (John 7:31)

Predictions of Jesus' Final Week

So far we've sampled prophecies that were fulfilled in Jesus' birth and ministry. Now let's zoom in on the week Jesus died. Here we see even more detailed predictions.

It was the week of the Passover feast, a time when great crowds of people were gathering in Jerusalem. "They heard that Jesus was on his way to Jerusalem. They took palm branches and went out to meet him, shouting, 'Hosannah! Blessed is he who comes in the name of the Lord! Blessed is the king of Israel!' Jesus found a young donkey and sat upon it" (John 12:12-14). He rode into Jerusalem on that donkey, surrounded by the cheering crowd.

This had been predicted in the Old Testament. Eight centuries earlier, a singer had written, "Blessed is he who comes in the name of the Lord... With branches in hand, join in the festal procession" (Psalm 118:26-27). More than 500 years earlier, the prophet Zechariah had written, "Rejoice greatly, O Daughter of Zion! Shout, Daughter of Jerusalem! See, your king comes to you, righteous and having salvation, gentle and riding on a donkey, on a colt, the foal of a donkey" (Zechariah 9:9). When Jesus climbed onto the young donkey and rode into Jerusalem, acclaimed by crowds with palm branches, it showed that he was the person the prophets predicted.

But these prophecies mentioned more than just a donkey ride and palm branches. Zechariah had gone on to say, "Because of the blood of my covenant with you, I will free your prisoners from the waterless pit" (9:11). The king on the donkey was going to bring freedom based on blood. He would be gentle, so he wasn't going to be shedding the blood of others. But if it wasn't going to be their blood, whose blood would it be? His own! According to Zechariah, the king on a donkey would somehow rescue others through his own blood.

Likewise, Psalm 118 spoke not only of praise and palm branches, but went on to say, "The stone the builders rejected has become the capstone; the Lord has done this, and it is marvelous in our eyes" (Psalm 118:22-23). As Jesus rode into Jerusalem, he knew what this ancient prophecy meant (see Matthew 21:42). He knew that "the builders," the main religious leaders, would reject and kill him. He also knew God would raise him up again and give him the highest position in the world.

Before going to his death, however, Jesus did some other things that fulfilled Old Testament prophecy. After riding into Jerusalem, Jesus went to the temple. The temple was supposed to have a court of the Gentiles, where people from any nation who wanted to worship the God of Israel could do so. But the religious leaders hated foreigners, and they were greedy for money, so they turned the court of the Gentiles into a currency exchange and a market for selling animals for the temple sacrifices. When Jesus saw this, he stormed into the temple, made a whip, and cleared out all the salesmen and money-grubbers.

450 years earlier, the prophet Malachi had written, "Then suddenly the Lord you are seeking will come to his temple... But

who can endure the day of his coming? Who can stand when he appears? For he will be like a refiner's fire or a launderer's soap" (Malachi 3:1-2). When the Lord Jesus came to his temple and cleaned it up, he was fulfilling that prophecy.

As he was driving out the money-grubbers, Jesus said, "'My house will be called a house of prayer,' but you are making it a 'den of robbers'" (Matthew 21:13). More than 700 years earlier, God had said through Isaiah, "My house will be called a house of prayer for all nations" (Isaiah 56:7). When Jesus cleared the merchants from the court of the Gentiles, he showed that he is the one who clears the way for true prayer and for people of all nations to have full access to God—just as Isaiah had prophesied.

When Jesus said the religious leaders had made his temple "a den of robbers," he was quoting the prophet Jeremiah (7:11). This prophet from six centuries earlier had spoken of "a den of robbers" in a prophecy about the temple. People in Jeremiah's day were treating the temple like a good luck charm that would keep them safe no matter what they did or how they related to God. But through Jeremiah, God said that since they had made God's temple a den of robbers, the temple wouldn't do them any good. God would destroy his temple and punish the nation. Shortly after Jeremiah's prophecy, the soldiers of Babylon came and reduced the temple to rubble.

Later, though, the temple was rebuilt, and by Jesus' day, it was again corrupt. So Jesus quoted from Jeremiah and called the temple a den of robbers. Jesus also took Jeremiah's prophecy of destruction and applied it once again. Jesus said that the temple would soon be reduced to rubble (Matthew 24:2). Less than forty years later, Jesus' words came true. Roman armies under Titus destroyed the temple, and to this day, it has never been rebuilt.

After Jesus cleaned out the temple, his enemies decided it was time to get rid of him. In the process, many more Old Testament predictions came true. The religious leaders paid Judas, a member of Jesus' inner circle, to betray him. This fulfilled Psalm 41:9, written a thousand years earlier, which said, "Even my close friend, whom I trusted, he who shared my bread, has lifted up his heel against me." When Jesus was arrested, his disciples all ran away, just as Jesus had said they would, and just as the prophet Zechariah had predicted long ago, "Strike the shepherd, and the sheep will be scattered" (13:7).

Jesus was dragged away, given a phony trial, and convicted. His enemies beat him, mocked him, and spit on him. Isaiah had foreseen this long before when he wrote, "I offered my back to those who beat me, my cheeks to those who pulled out my beard; I did not hide my face from mocking and spitting" (50:6).

Predictions of Death and Resurrection

The manner of Jesus' torture and death revealed him as the one the prophets predicted. Long ago Psalm 22 had said, "They have pierced my hands and my feet... They divide my garments among them and cast lots for my clothing." A thousand years later soldiers pounded spikes through Jesus' hands and feet and gambled to see which of them would get his clothing. Psalm 22 says, "My God, my God, why have you forsaken me?" A thousand years later Jesus cried those very words as he hung on the cross. Psalm 22 speaks of mockery and of people sneering, "He trusts in the Lord; let the Lord rescue him." A thousand years later, Jesus' enemies said: "Let him come down now from the cross and we will believe in him. *He trusts in God. Let God rescue him* now if he wants him, for he said, 'I am the Son of God'" (Matthew 27:43). Psalm 22 said, "My tongue sticks to the roof of my mouth." A thousand years later the dying Jesus cried, "I am thirsty" (John 19:28). Psalm 69 said, "They gave me vinegar for my thirst." A thousand years later someone offered the cruci- fied Jesus wine vinegar to drink (John 19:29).

When Jesus died, the treatment of his body fulfilled ancient prophecies. It was the day before the Sabbath, and the people in charge wanted to make sure Jesus and the two men crucified with him were dead before sundown. So the soldiers broke the legs of the two criminals crucified with Jesus. With broken legs, they wouldn't be able to hold up their weight and would soon die from not being able to get air in their lungs. The soldiers intended to break Jesus' legs too, but when they found he was already dead, they left his legs alone and simply pierced Jesus' side with a spear to make sure. Centuries earlier the Old Testament had said, "Not one of his bones will be broken" (Exodus 12:46, Psalm 34:20). Another scripture had said, "They will look on the one they have pierced" (Zechariah 12:10). Then a rich man named Joseph of Arimathea laid Jesus' body to rest in a tomb Joseph had purchased for his own burial. This fulfilled what Isaiah had said long ago, "He was assigned a grave with the wicked, and with the rich in his death" (Isaiah 53:9).

Even the timing of all this showed that Jesus was the person the prophets predicted. Jesus died during Passover week. Back in the time of Moses, the angel of death killed the firstborn of Egypt and rescued the Israelites from slavery. Each Israelite household was passed over and spared if the blood of a lamb was smeared on the doorpost of the home. The lamb died instead of the firstborn son, and its blood saved God's people from death (Exodus 11-12). Each year Passover marked that event.

Jesus died at the very time when Passover week was reaching its climax. Jesus is the ultimate Passover, the final sacrifice. Fourteen centuries earlier the slaughtered Passover lamb and the liberation from Egypt had been the foreshadowing. The slaughtering of Jesus, the Lamb of God, and the great liberation from sin and Satan that Jesus' death achieved—this was the fulfillment. The timing of the Passover and the crucifixion matched perfectly, again linking the ancient Scriptures with the person of Jesus.

How could so many prophecies turn out to be so accurate? And how could one person be the fulfillment of all those things which were written so many years earlier? The answer is simply that these predictions in the Old Testament were promises from God, and that this Jesus is the One God sent to save us. How else could the person and the predictions match so precisely?

Old Testament predictions didn't stop at the death of the Messiah. Psalm 16:10 said, "You will not abandon me to the grave, nor will you let your Holy One see decay." Isaiah 53:11 said, "After the suffering of his soul, he will see the light of life and be satisfied; by his knowledge my righteous servant will justify many." Psalm 22 said that after being forsaken by God and pierced by men, the afflicted one would live and rejoice and bring far-off nations to the Lord. Sure enough, Jesus didn't stay in the grave, and his body didn't decay. He rose from the dead, saw the light of life, and has brought joy, salvation and eternal life to people from many nations ever since.

Reason to Believe

So if you ask, "Why be a Christian and not something else? Why believe the Bible and not some other book? Why trust Jesus and not some other person?" the answer is that there is no other book like the Bible, and there is no other person like Jesus. The Bible is God speaking in written form, and Jesus is God living among us in human form.

Before you believe in some other book that claims to be from God, be sure to ask whether that book accurately predicted things long in advance of when they happened. Before you believe in some other religious leader, be sure to ask how many prophecies he fulfills, and ask whether he died and was buried and then walked out of the tomb alive. No book but the Bible reveals God's promises even before they come true. No person but Jesus fulfills all those promises. No religious leader is holy and loving enough to die for the sins of his people, and no religious leader is mighty enough to conquer death and Satan.

This is what the New Testament calls "the gospel God promised beforehand through his prophets in the Holy Scriptures regarding his Son" (Romans 1:2-3). This is why someone who met Jesus exclaimed, "We have found the one Moses wrote about in the Law, and about whom the prophets also wrote" (John 1:45). This is why Jesus himself said, "Everything must be fulfilled that is written about me in the Law of Moses, the Prophets and the Psalms" (Luke 24:44).

There may still be a lot you don't know about the Bible and a lot you don't understand about Jesus, but when you see how the Bible and Jesus fit one another perfectly, you at least know what book you can believe as God's Word and what person you can trust as God's Son. Don't let the variety of religious books and religious leaders confuse you or keep you from making up your mind. Other books may contain valuable insights, but the Bible is God's book. Other leaders may have their good points, but Jesus is God's Son. Believe the Bible, and study it more and more. Trust Jesus, and get to know him better and better.

Chapter 7

Jesus' Deity Displayed

There's more to some people than meets the eye. You may think you know someone and yet not see who they really are or what they're able to do. Someone who grew up on your street becomes a famous author, and you exclaim, "I didn't know she had it in her!" Someone you knew as just another kid in your college dorm ends up running a giant corporation, and you say, "Wow! I'd never have guessed it!" If you grow up with people or see them a lot, you feel you know them, and you tend to think they're pretty ordinary. Even when they do astonishing things, it may still be hard to believe they're all that great.

If it's hard to believe that someone you're familiar with turned out to have hidden talents, how hard would it be to believe that a guy who grew up in your hometown is actually God?

Jesus grew up in the town of Nazareth. His neighbors thought they knew him pretty well. They thought they knew his family pretty well. They saw him grow up with the other kids of the town. They saw him working with wood in a carpenter shop.

But about the time Jesus turned thirty, he left his quiet, ordinary life in Nazareth and began preaching and doing miracles in some of the towns nearby. Stories about Jesus began drifting back to his hometown, and the people of Nazareth were shocked. They must have thought, "This man Jesus, a brilliant teacher with miraculous powers? Come on! How can that be? We've known this guy since he was in diapers! We've watched him play. We've heard him cry. We've seen him sawing wood. He had sweat on his forehead and dirt under his fingernails, just like anyone else who works with his hands."

It was hard to believe Jesus was anybody special, but rumors about his preaching and marvelous miracles kept floating back to Nazareth. Then one day Jesus came back. The local people were eager to find out if the hometown boy was really as great as the rumors claimed. They crowded into their meeting place, the synagogue, to hear him. When he spoke, they were amazed. He really surprised them—they had to admit it. But then their old mental habits and their feeling of familiarity took over.

"Where did this man get this wisdom and these miraculous powers?" they asked. "Isn't this the carpenter's son? Isn't his mother's name Mary, and aren't his brothers James, Joseph, Simon and Judas? Aren't his sisters all with us? Where then did this man get all these things?" And they were offended at him (Matthew 13:54-56).

The people of Nazareth knew exactly what Jesus looked like, and his looks didn't impress them. They knew his family, and his family didn't impress them. "No doubt about it," figured the hometown folks. "This man Jesus is as human as any of us; he's nobody special." They were right that Jesus is as human as anyone. But they were wrong to think he's nobody special. They were so busy seeing Jesus as one of them that they couldn't see him as anything more.

The people of Nazareth weren't the only ones who had trouble recognizing Jesus as God. For a while his own brothers did not believe in him (John 7:5), and his disciples weren't always sure what to make of Jesus. They saw something special in Jesus, but it didn't sink in right away that this man they loved and admired so much was actually God as well as a man.

Once, when Jesus was talking privately with his friends, he said, "If you really knew me, you would know my Father as well. From now on, you do know him and have seen him" (John 14:7). That statement baffled Jesus' friends. They had often heard Jesus speak of God as his Father, but what could he mean by saying they already knew the Father and had seen him?

One of the disciples, Philip, blurted out, "Lord, show us the Father and that will be enough for us" (John 14:8). Philip was asking for a direct display of who God is. "If only we could see him, if only you'd show him to us, then we would know God."

Jesus answered: "Don't you know me, Philip, even after I have been among you such a long time? Anyone who has seen me has seen the Father. How can you say, 'Show us the Father'? Don't you believe that I am in the Father, and that the Father is in me" (John 14:9-10)? Jesus was saying, "You're asking me to show you God? Open your eyes! Don't you recognize me? *If you've seen me, you've seen God.*"

But, you might wonder, how could the disciples be expected to recognize God in the face of this carpenter/teacher? And how can we be expected to recognize Jesus as divine? Jesus pointed out two kinds of evidence that should make it obvious: *his words* and *his works.* Jesus said, "The words I say to you are not just my own. Rather, it is the Father, living in me, who is doing his work" (John 14:10). Jesus' words aren't just a man's words but God's words. So we ought to believe Jesus is God on the sheer authority of what he says. And if we don't sense the divine authority of his words, we still ought to see him as God on the basis of his miracles and the divine power displayed in them. Jesus said, "Believe me when I say that I am in the Father and the Father is in me; or at least believe on the evidence of the miracles themselves" (John 14:11).

Nobody who met Jesus had any doubt that he was completely human. And yet... and yet... there was something more than human about him. He went around saying things only God could say and doing things only God could do. The truth about Jesus is this: Jesus is just as human as you or I, and at the same time he is just as divine as God the Father.

That's the truth, but not everyone back then believed it, and still today, not everyone believes it. Some folks don't pay much attention to Jesus or see anything special about him. Others, such as Jehovah's Witnesses and Muslims, think Jesus was a special man but don't think he's God. Even some supposedly Christian people may view Jesus as a great man and a superb example but can't accept that Jesus is God. If you're one of those who don't see Jesus as God, or if you ever talk with others who think that way, keep reading. We'll see how the words and works of Jesus show him to be God. Jesus seemed like just an ordinary man, but he talked like God and acted like God. His words rang with divine authority, and his works displayed divine power. Let's take a closer look, first at his words, and then at his works.

Talking Like God

There was something striking about Jesus' words, about what he said, how he said it, and the impact on his listeners. Jesus could speak shrewdly but simply. He had amazing insight into deep truths, yet he could teach these things in simple words and gripping stories. When highly educated experts tried to question him and stump him or trap him into saying something foolish, he always had the perfect answer. The smartest people couldn't outwit him, yet the simplest people could benefit from his teaching. Jesus' simple brilliance left people scratching their heads in amazement. Even those who didn't like him had to wonder, "How did this man get such learning without having studied?" (John 7:15)

Whenever Jesus spoke, people were stunned by his intellect and insight; they were also amazed by the sheer authority of how he spoke. He wasn't like other teachers who were constantly debating the fine points of religion. Those people spoke as specialists and scholars. Someone has defined scholars as people who learn more and more about less and less until they know almost everything about almost nothing. By that definition, the religious teachers of Jesus' day were scholars indeed. They specialized in trivia and knew almost everything about almost nothing. They didn't see the big picture, and when they spoke, it wasn't with any true sense of authority. If they wanted to prove a point, they usually just piled up quotes from other scholars.

How different when Jesus spoke! The Bible says that when Jesus finished preaching his great Sermon on the Mount, "The crowds were amazed at his teaching, because he taught as one who had authority, and not as their teachers of the law" (Matthew 7:29). Jesus didn't base his teaching on scholarly opinion; he did the opposite. "You have heard it said [by your experts]," Jesus would say as he introduced a subject, "but *I* tell you"—and then, *on his own authority*, he would declare the real truth of the matter. Over and over Jesus contradicted prevailing opinions and declared what God really was saying. As Jesus preached the Sermon on the Mount, his voice rang with the same authority as the voice that had thundered out the Ten Commandments on Mount Sinai. It was the voice of God.

Jesus' brilliant teaching and his sense of authority were enough to astonish even those who didn't quite know what to make of him. Once the chief priests and Pharisees sent some security guards to arrest Jesus while he was speaking in the temple. But the guards—those tough, no-nonsense enforcers—were stunned by Jesus' wisdom and air of authority, and they couldn't bring themselves to arrest him.

"Finally the temple guards went back to the chief priests and the Pharisees, who asked them, "Why didn't you bring him in?"

"No one ever spoke the way this man does," the guards declared (John 7:45-46).

No one ever spoke as Jesus spoke, and no one ever dared to say the things Jesus said. Once Jesus was having dinner in the home of a religious man when a woman who had lived a very sinful life came into the house. Jesus said to her, "Your sins are forgiven." The other guests in the house were shocked. They said among themselves, "Who is this that even forgives sins?" (See Luke 7:36-50)

Good question! "Who is this that even forgives sins?" No mere human can forgive sins committed against other people. That sinful woman had probably damaged a number of marriages by her immorality. She may have spread sexually transmitted diseases. If she had children, they undoubtedly had been harmed by her evil behavior. But whatever marriages she wrecked, whatever men she infected, whatever children she neglected, whoever else she hurt, what did that have to do with Jesus? If Jesus was not the one she wronged, then he was not the one to forgive her. How could he say, "Your sins are forgiven"? He couldn't—unless he is the main one offended, the God whose law is broken and whose love is wounded in every sin. Jesus' words of forgiveness were words that only God could speak.

Jesus went around talking like he was God. His deity was implicit in all his words, and Jesus was also explicit in saying he was God. Jesus told his friends, "Anyone who has seen me has seen the Father" (John 14:9). He told his enemies, "I and the Father are one" (John 10:30). When he said that, his enemies picked up stones to kill him, complaining it was blasphemy, "because you, a mere man, claim to be God" (John 10:33). These people were wrong not to believe Jesus, but they were certainly right that he was openly claiming to be God.

That's the first reason we should believe Jesus is God: because he says so! His words—his superhuman insight, his stunning authority, his amazing claims to forgive sins and to be one with God—ring with divine authority.

Acting Like God

Jesus didn't just talk like God; he acted like God. Jesus told his friends, "Believe me when I say that I am in the Father and the Father is in me; or at least believe on the evidence of the miracles themselves." Jesus said much the same thing to his enemies: "Why do you accuse me of blasphemy because I said, 'I am God's Son'? ...[Even] though you do not believe me, believe the miracles, that you may know and understand that the Father is in me, and I in the Father" (John 10:36-38).

"Believe the miracles!" Have you ever simply read through the New Testament gospels—Matthew, Mark, Luke, and John? If not, do so. Look at the things Jesus did. Look at the sheer number of miracles and the difficulty of those miracles. How could anyone but God do such things? Jesus drove out demons and walked on water. He gave sight to the blind, hearing to the deaf, speech to the mute, movement to the paralyzed, life to the dead! Even before any careful study of the meaning of each individual miracle, the overall impact of seeing the things Jesus did is an overwhelming sense of supernatural, divine power.

If the overall impression of Jesus' works still doesn't convince you that he's God, then take a closer look at some details. Look at a few specific miracles of Jesus in the New Testament gospels, and notice how they match the work of God Almighty described in the Old Testament.

The gospels tell of a time when Jesus and his disciples were out on a lake in a small boat. A furious storm came up, and waves were sweeping over the boat. Jesus' friends were terrified. They feared that they were about to drown. But what did Jesus do? He spoke to the wind and the waves and said, "Quiet! Be still!" The storm hushed and the sea became calm. Jesus' disciples exclaimed, "Who is this? Even the wind and the waves obey him!" (Mark 4:37-41)

Who is this? For the answer to that question, look in the Old Testament. Psalm 89:8-9 says, "O Lord God Almighty, who is like you? ... You rule over the surging sea; when its waves mount up, you still them." Only God Almighty can still stormy seas. So if Jesus stilled a stormy sea, who is he? He is God Almighty!

Or look at two other well-known miracles of Jesus in the New Testament gospels. Once, when Jesus was a guest at a wedding, he turned water into wine (John 2:1-11). On another occasion, Jesus changed five loaves of bread into enough food for a multitude of thousands (Mark 6:34-44).

What does this say about Jesus? In the Old Testament Psalm 104 says, "O Lord my God, you are very great" (104:1) and speaks of God's work in creation. Among other things, Psalm 104 mentions specifically that the Creator provides "*wine* that gladdens the heart of man ... and *bread* that sustains his heart" (104:15). So when Jesus turned water into wine, and when he miraculously gave bread to a crowd of more than five thousand, what did it mean? It meant he is the Maker of heaven and earth and the great supplier of all food and drink.

Let's look at another example of a miracle of Jesus that fits the way the Lord God is described in the Old Testament. Psalm

103 says, "Praise the Lord, O my soul ... who forgives all your sins and heals all your diseases" (103:2-3). Only God can forgive all sins. Only God can heal all diseases.

The New Testament gospels tell of Jesus forgiving sins and healing diseases. One particular story makes this especially clear. Some men came to Jesus carrying a paralyzed man on a mat. Jesus was in a house, and it was too crowded for them to get in, so they climbed up on top of the house, tore a hole in the roof, and lowered the mat the paralyzed man was lying on. When Jesus saw the faith of this man and his friends, he said, "Son; your sins are forgiven."

> Now some teachers of the law were sitting there, thinking to themselves, "Why does this fellow talk like that? He's blaspheming! Who can forgive sins but God alone?"
>
> Immediately Jesus knew in his spirit that this was what they were thinking in their hearts, and he said to them, "Why are you thinking these things? Which is easier: to say to the paralytic, 'Your sins are forgiven,' or to say, 'Get up, take your mat and walk'? But so that you may know that the Son of Man has authority on earth to forgive sins..." He said to the paralytic, "I tell you, get up, take your mat, and go home." He got up, took his mat and walked out in full view of them all. This amazed everyone and they praised God, saying, "We have never seen anything like this!"

Psalm 103 praises God "who forgives all your sins and heals all your diseases," so the religious teachers had a biblical basis for saying that only God can forgive sins. When Jesus said, "Son, your sins are forgiven," he was saying what only God could say. When his opponents challenged him, Jesus responded by doing what only God could do: he healed incurable paralysis. Jesus showed that he is the God who not only forgives sins but also the God who heals all diseases. His work of healing confirmed his word of forgiveness, and both confirmed his identity as God.

You might wonder if the Bible exaggerates Jesus' miracles, but it does the opposite. The Bible doesn't exaggerate; instead, it leaves out most of Jesus' miracles. The miracles described in the Bible are stunning, but they're only a sample. "Jesus did many other miraculous signs in the presence of his disciples which are not recorded in this book" (John 20:30). The biblical authors didn't write all the amazing things Jesus did. But under God's guidance, they wrote enough to get the main point across and show that Jesus is God. "These are written that you may believe that Jesus is the Christ, the Son of God, and that by believing you may have life in his name" (John 20:31).

Liar, Lunatic, or Lord?

Jesus talked and acted like God. So you can't just think that he's an inspired prophet or a wise teacher. You either have to accept Jesus as Savior and Lord, or else you have to reject him as wicked or wacky. It's all or nothing. C. S. Lewis writes,

> There is no half-way house and there is no parallel in other religions. If you had gone to Buddha and asked him 'Are you the son of Brahma?' he would have said, 'My son, you are still in the vale of illusion.' If you had gone to Socrates and asked, 'Are you Zeus?' he would have laughed at you. If you had gone to Mohammed and asked, "Are you Allah?' he would first have rent his clothes and then cut your head off. If you had asked Confucius, 'Are you Heaven?', I think he would have probably replied, 'Remarks which are not in accordance with nature are in bad taste.' The idea of a great moral teacher saying what Christ said is out of the question... We may note in passing that Jesus was never regarded as a mere moral teacher. He did not produce that effect on any of the people who actually met Him. He produced mainly three effects—Hatred—Terror—Adoration. There was no trace of people expressing mild approval.

These days, however, some people do express mild approval of Jesus. Maybe that's your reaction. You don't adore and obey Jesus as God or trust him as the only one who can save you from sin and hell. But you don't really want to say anything bad about

Jesus either. So your reaction to Jesus is mild approval. You say he's a wise prophet or spiritual teacher or brave rebel. But if that's what you say, you're simply ignoring what Jesus himself says.

Suppose I introduce myself to you and say, "Hi, my name is David Feddes. I was educated in a seminary, and now I'm a preacher." You say, "Nice to meet you, Mr. Lettuce. I'm glad you're dedicated to a cemetery where flowers are a feature. We need people like you to keep our graveyards beautiful." At that point, I'm not going to say, "I'm glad you appreciate me." No, I'm going to say, "You didn't hear me right. My name isn't Lettuce, it's Feddes: F-E-D-D-E-S. And I didn't say I'm dedicated to a cemetery where flowers are a feature. I said I was educated in a seminary, and now I am a preacher."

A misunderstanding like that may sound silly, but it's no sillier than hearing Jesus claim to forgive sins and to be God with us and then saying, "Glad to meet you, Jesus. You say you're a good teacher with some helpful spiritual ideas? I think that's great, and I may even want to use a few of your ideas myself." At that point I can almost hear Jesus saying, "Did I say I'm just a good teacher? No, I claimed authority to forgive sins. Did I say I was offering you some helpful ideas about God and that you can pick and choose which ones you like? No, I said that I am one with God and that I give eternal life to all who believe in me." Let me quote C.S. Lewis again:

A man who was merely a man and said the sort of things Jesus said would not be a great moral teacher. He would either be a lunatic—on a level with a man who says he is a poached egg—or else he would be the Devil of Hell. You must make your choice. Either this man was, and is, the Son of God: or else a madman or something worse. You can shut Him up for a fool, you can spit at him and kill him as a demon; or you can fall at his feet and call Him Lord and God. But let us not come with any patronizing nonsense about His being a great human teacher. He has not left that open to us. He did not intend to.

Jesus leaves no room for half-baked thinking, no room for half-hearted action. You must make up your mind and then act accordingly. The Lord Almighty has lived and walked among us. Believe Jesus' words. Believe his works.

Believe the most stunning word and the most stunning work of all: Jesus first said he would rise from the dead, and then he did it! Who but God could speak such a word? Who but God could do such a work? Who but God is stronger than death?

Chapter 8

Tall Tales About Jesus

Jesus is such a gripping figure that all sorts of stories exist about him. A place in northern Japan claims to be the spot where Jesus is buried. Harold Netland, an expert on world religions and long-time resident of Japan, tells what the local legend says about Jesus:

> After growing up in Galilee [in northern Israel], Jesus came to Japan before beginning his public ministry. He returned to Galilee at age thirty-three and began preaching a heavenly kingdom: namely, Japan. When he encountered trouble with the Jewish leaders, Jesus left Galilee and returned to the town of Shingo, near beautiful Lake Towada. According to the legend, Jesus' brother, Isukiri, was crucified in Jesus' place on the cross. Jesus lived in northern Japan until his death at age 106. Local townsfolk point out the grave where he was supposedly buried.

Should we believe what those Japanese villagers say about Jesus instead of what the Bible says? Of course not. The gospel accounts in the Bible were all written in the first century. This is confirmed by analysis of ancient manuscripts. Not even the most skeptical analysts deny that all four New Testament gospels about the life of Jesus were written within the lifetime of people who knew Jesus. In contrast, the story in the Japanese village is just a local legend that somehow sprang up centuries later and cannot compare with the historical accounts of Jesus.

People of many different places and religions have their own ideas about Jesus. Few reject Jesus outright or believe nothing at

all about him. Many Hindu shrines and homes include an image
of Jesus. Some Hindus fit Jesus to Hindu thinking and make
him an avatar or one among the millions of Hindu gods, not the
only Son of the only God, as Jesus declared himself to be.

Some Buddhists, such as the Dalai Lama, see Jesus as a fully
enlightened being or as a high-level *bodhisattva* whose aim was to
share Buddhist enlightenment with others, not as the Savior who
died for our sins and rose again that we might also receive immortal resurrection bodies.

Muslim writings, produced more than 600 years after Jesus'
death and resurrection, say that Jesus was a prophet. However,
they insist that Jesus did not claim to be God's Son. They also
claim that Jesus was not crucified, because God would not let his
prophet suffer such pain and disgrace. Someone else—Judas—
was made to look like Jesus and was crucified. Jesus went directly
to heaven, and will return to judge the world and establish Islam.

The Ahmadiyya sect of Islam says Jesus was crucified but did
not die. He only swooned. Jesus revived in the cool tomb and
was cured of his wounds by a special ointment. Jesus fled Pales-
tine and journeyed toward India, to what is today Kashmir. He
later died naturally of old age and was buried there. You can visit
the alleged place of his burial and donate money.

The book of Mormon, written by an American 1800 years
after the New Testament, claims that Jesus came to peoples living in America. Mormonism also teaches that God the Father
has a physical body and that Jesus was produced by a physical
union of God and Mary.

To know the real Jesus, you can't believe every tall tale
someone tells about him, and you can't make up your own version of Jesus. You have to listen to the eyewitness accounts of
those who saw and heard him. Only the New Testament books
contain what Jesus' friends heard him say and saw him do.

The Gospel of Judas

The Gospel of Judas differs from the New Testament gospels
of Matthew, Mark, Luke, and John. The Gospel of Judas claims

to reveal the real Jesus and the real Judas. The real Judas, according to this ancient document, was not evil. Instead, Judas was the only one of the twelve apostles who really understood Jesus. Jesus secretly told Judas his real message. Jesus taught Judas that the physical world is evil, that bodies are bad, and that people have an inner divine being. This divine self needs to escape the prison of the body in order to fulfill its divine destiny.

When Judas handed Jesus over to his enemies to be killed, it was not a wicked betrayal; the Gospel of Judas says that Jesus ordered Judas to do it. Jesus told Judas that he would surpass all the other disciples, because Judas would help Jesus to escape his body and become pure spirit. Jesus told Judas, "You will sacrifice the man that clothes me." According to the gospel of Judas, Jesus did not die to get rid of the world's sin; he died to get rid of his own body. Jesus did not rise from the dead in a glorified resurrection body, and he did not promise that his followers would be physically raised from the dead. Bodily resurrection would be tragedy, not triumph. Bodies are bad!

That contradicts what the Bible says. According to the New Testament gospels, Judas was not the best of all the apostles but the worst. He was a thief and a traitor. Judas was a member of Jesus' ministry team, and one of his duties was to serve as treasurer. But Judas stole money that people had given for God's work. Eventually Judas became so greedy that he decided to go for one big payday. He went to Jesus' enemies and offered to betray Jesus to them for a payment of thirty silver coins. Satan, the chief of demons, entered Judas's heart, and Judas did Satan's work. He led a band of men armed with swords and clubs through the darkness of night to the place he knew Jesus would be. Judas gave Jesus a kiss, not out of love, but to help Jesus' enemies pick Jesus out of the crowd and seize him. Afterward Satan had no further use for Judas. Judas was filled with horror and killed himself. That's what the Bible says about Judas.

As for Jesus and his message, the Bible never says Jesus told people that they have a divine inner self that needs to be free of the body. It is not bad to have a body; the Bible says God created bodies. When Jesus died, it was not to get rid of his body but to get rid of our sin. Jesus did not just dwell in a spirit realm. He arose from the dead in a body that could be seen and touched. When Jesus returns, he will raise our bodies.

The gospels in the Bible say one thing; the gospel of Judas says another. What should we believe? When the Judas manuscript came to light, the news media gave it lots of publicity. You may have heard people say that the gospel of Judas is a legitimate alternative to the Bible. You may have heard that experts authenticate the gospel of Judas as very old.

Granted, it is old—but not old enough. It goes back many centuries—but not as far back as the biblical gospels. The Bible's accounts were written within a few decades of Jesus death and resurrection by people who knew Jesus personally. The Judas manuscript, on the other hand, is dated about 150 years after Judas betrayed Jesus. 150 years is a long time. The author did not know Jesus or Judas. The book was written by Gnostics who thought bodies were bad. Some Gnostics called themselves Cainites. They admired not only Judas but Cain, the biblical character who murdered his brother Abel. This cult twisted almost everything the Bible said into its opposite and turned many villains into heroes.

Let's imagine a different example of writing a book 150 years after events, a book that contradicts the historical accounts of eyewitnesses. It's been roughly 150 years since President Abraham Lincoln was shot. Suppose somebody sat down today and wrote a book titled *History of Booth*. Suppose this book claimed to give the real, hidden story behind Abraham Lincoln's death. *History of Booth* claimed that Lincoln secretly told John Wilkes Booth to shoot him, and the assassin Booth was actually an American hero. Now imagine that the person who wrote this book was part of a group called the Arnoldites, named after Benedict Arnold, the traitorous general who worked for America's enemy. Would you take seriously a book that said the secret of being a true American is to follow in the footsteps of Benedict Arnold, the traitor who double-crossed George Washington, and

John Wilkes Booth, the assassin who murdered Abraham Lincoln? Who would believe such ridiculous lies dreamed up long after the actual events?

If such a *History of Booth* would be ridiculous, the Gospel of Judas is even more ridiculous. But some journalists and professors act as though it reveals things that place the biblical gospels in question.

The Da Vinci Code

A similar dynamic occurred with the ridiculous Gnostic ideas described in *The Da Vinci Code*. Tell a big enough lie often enough to lots of people, and eventually some of them believe it. *The Da Vinci Code* is a mystery novel that sold millions of copies and made millions of dollars for author Dan Brown. Like any popular mystery, *The Da Vinci Code* offers many plot twists and secrets. The main mystery of the novel, the deepest secret it claims to reveal, is the secret of the real Jesus.

According to the novel, "almost everything our fathers taught us about Christ is wrong." When the mystery of Jesus is solved, it turns out that Jesus got married. He and his wife, Mary Magdalene, produced offspring. These offspring were taken to France and became part of a royal line.

According to the novelist, Jesus was not really God come to earth as a human. Rather, church leaders made up the deity of Christ a few hundred years after Jesus died. These leaders wanted to increase their own power, so they declared Christ to be God and poured their efforts into hiding the real truth.

The Council of Nicea, meeting in 325, declared Jesus to be the only begotten Son of God, the second person of the divine Trinity. "Until that moment in history," says the author of *The Da Vinci Code*, "Jesus was viewed by his followers as a mortal prophet... a great and powerful man, but a *man* nonetheless."

Dan Brown's mystery story has entertained millions of readers, and a film version entertained millions of moviegoers. If you read the book or see the movie, keep in mind that what you're getting is fiction, not fact. However, Dan Brown claims to offer more than fiction. The book claims, "All descriptions of ... documents ... in this novel are accurate." *The Da Vinci Code* is more than an effort to entertain people and make money. It is an effort to promote a view of Jesus that differs from the Bible and the Christian church. It is a deliberate attack on what Christians for many centuries have believed about Jesus.

Dan Brown claims that Jesus' earliest followers saw him as just a great man and only in later centuries did some people make up the idea that Jesus is God as well as man. But Brown has it backward. The Bible books were written by eyewitnesses within a few decades of Jesus' time on earth; the writings Dan Brown refers to were produced long afterward by deviant groups that had no personal connection with Jesus. Jesus' earliest friends and followers heard him claim to be God as well as man, and they made this clear in the writings of the Bible. Only later did others make up a different Jesus and write new stories denying Jesus' deity and contradicting the original facts of the Bible.

The Da Vinci Code claims to be based on real documents from the past that speak about Jesus. Some of those documents still exist, but they are tall tales people came up with long after the time of Jesus. All sorts of stories and ideas have sprung up about Jesus in the centuries after he came. That doesn't make them as trustworthy as the biblical writings produced by those who actually saw and heard the real Jesus.

A Trustworthy Source

The Bible book of John was written by Jesus' closest friend, his dearest disciple. John was not a novelist eager to sell books and make money. John knew Jesus personally, loved him dearly, related to Jesus as God the Son, and wanted others to relate to Jesus as God the Son. John 20:31 explains the book's main purpose: "These are written that you may believe that Jesus is the Christ, the Son of God, and that by believing you may have life in his name" (John 20:31).

Contrary to Dan Brown's tall tales about Jesus in *The Da Vinci Code*, the earliest Christians, including Jesus' closest friend,

knew Jesus as the Son of God. When the Council of Nicea declared that Jesus is divine along with the Father and the Holy
Spirit, the Council was not making up something new. It was
restating what John and Jesus' other friends, the authors of the
New Testament, had been saying all along. The Council was re-
affirming the deity of Jesus and the truth of the Trinity to coun-
teract false ideas cooked up by a renegade leader named Arius. It
was not just the council of Nicea 300 years later which spoke of
Jesus as God. All four gospels show Jesus saying what only God
could say and doing what only God could do. In John's gospel,
it was an eyewitness to Jesus' resurrection who called Jesus "My
Lord and my God" (John 20:28).

If you don't want to accept Jesus as God, you can always find
a way out. You can reject the New Testament, and you can focus
on stories and ideas written long afterward. You can even dream
up things on your own and write a novel, such as *The Da Vinci
Code*. You can say whatever you want to say about Jesus—but
that doesn't change the truth.

The truth about Jesus is that he was and is God and man. He
came into this world to show us God's love, to die as a sacrifice
to pay for our sins, and to defeat death through his resurrection
and return to glory. The biblical truth about Mary Magdalene
(the woman alleged in *The Da Vinci Code* to be Jesus' wife) is
that Jesus saved Mary Magdalene from demons that possessed
her. Mary loved Jesus as her Savior and friend, not as her husband. Mary Magdalene was the first to see Jesus alive after his
resurrection, but she never had children with him. If you've got
your own agenda, you can make up any fiction you like. But Jesus doesn't change with every tall tale, and truth doesn't change
with every popular novel.

The New Testament writers are authors we can trust. John
emphasized the difference between the phonies who never knew
Jesus and his own firsthand connection with Christ. John wrote,
"That which was from the beginning, which we have heard,
which we have seen with our eyes, which we have looked at and
our hands have touched—this we proclaim concerning the Word

of life" (1 John 1:1). Another New Testament writer, Jesus' dear friend Peter, made the same point: "We did not follow cleverly invented stories when we told you about the power and coming of our Lord Jesus Christ, but we were eyewitnesses of his majesty" (2 Peter 1:16).

The New Testament eyewitnesses were trustworthy people who spoke from firsthand experience. On top of that, they had God's inspiration and guidance to make them totally trustworthy in everything they wrote about Jesus. If the choice comes down to the *Gospel of Judas* or the Bible, believe the Bible. If the choice comes down to *The Da Vinci Code* or the Bible, believe the Bible. If the choice comes down to another religion's view of Jesus or the Bible's firsthand account, believe the Bible. Don't believe tall tales. Believe those who saw Jesus with their own eyes, heard him with their own ears, and wrote as he directed them.

Chapter 9

Dead or Alive?

If you've been wondering whether Christianity is something you should take seriously, it all comes down to one question: Is Jesus dead or alive? You may have other questions about the Christian faith, but those questions can wait. First make up your mind whether Jesus is dead or alive. If you conclude he's dead, you won't need to bother with other questions; you can forget about Christianity altogether. But if you conclude that Jesus is alive, you'll want to be a Christian, no matter what your other questions might be.

Sometimes we make things more complicated than they really are, but this isn't complicated at all. At this very moment, Jesus is alive and strong in an immortal resurrection body, or else he's nothing but dust. If Jesus is alive, you should be a Christian. If he's dead, you shouldn't be a Christian. It's that simple.

Perhaps this isn't the way you think of religion. You may think in terms of opinions and feelings, not physical facts. You may say things like, "It doesn't matter what you believe, as long as you're sincere about it" or "What you believe is true for you, and what I believe is true for me."

But the truth is this: if the resurrection didn't happen, if Jesus is dead and his body is decayed, then Christianity is false—it's not true for you or for me or for anyone else. It's not a question of feelings; it's a question of fact. If Jesus isn't alive, you can have all the feelings and opinions you want, but it won't change the fact that Jesus is dead and Christian faith is worthless. You and I need to know the physical facts.

Unlike what some religions offer, Christianity isn't just spiritual; it's also physical. Christians believe that God became flesh in the person of Jesus. We believe that after Jesus was crucified and buried, his dead body arose to glorious, unending life. We believe that certain women talked with him and even touched him after his resurrection. We believe that the risen Jesus spoke with his disciples, broke bread with them, and even ate broiled fish with them. We believe that today Jesus' immortal resurrection body is physically present in heaven. We believe that he will someday return to earth visibly, raise all his people in splendid, immortal bodies, and transform the entire physical universe to flourish forever, free of suffering and death. These are definite, physical claims. If they're not true, the Christian faith doesn't deserve your attention. The Bible says,

> If Christ has not been raised, our preaching is useless and so is your faith. More than that, we are then found to be false witnesses about God, for we have testified about God that he raised Christ from the dead... If Christ has not been raised, your faith is futile; you are still in your sins. Then those also who have fallen asleep in Christ are lost. If only for this life we have hope in Christ, we are to be pitied more than all men. But Christ has indeed been raised from the dead (1 Corinthians 15:14-20).

What Difference Does It Make?

What difference does it make if Jesus is dead or alive? Let's consider four things, each starting with the letter *F*: foundation, forgiveness, future, and fulfillment.

1. Foundation

The foundation of Christian faith depends on Jesus' resurrection. If Christ has not been raised, Christianity has no solid ground to stand on. If Christ is dead, the apostles were liars, and the New Testament belongs in the garbage. If Christ is dead, the apostles were false witnesses about God, for they "testified about God that he raised Christ from the dead," which is a lie if it never really happened. And if the apostles are liars, it means that the New Testament itself is a web of lies, since it is the written record of the apostles' testimony.

If Christ has not been raised, then the founder of Christianity, Jesus himself, was a liar—or somewhat of a lunatic. After all, Jesus claimed to be equal with God. He predicted that he would die for the sins of his people and then be raised again by the power of God. Obviously, if Jesus didn't overcome death, he was wrong and wasn't God at all. In that case, this man who claimed to be God was either a deceiver or else someone who wasn't in his right mind. Either way, it would be foolish to pay any attention to him.

However, if Jesus has been raised, if he's alive right now, then the situation is completely reversed: the foundations of Christianity are firm and immovable. If Jesus has been raised, then he was and is exactly who he claimed to be—the almighty Son of God. What's more, his hand-picked apostles who testified as eyewitnesses to his resurrection are trustworthy, and we should believe every word God inspired them to write. If Jesus is alive then the New Testament is rock-solid and reliable, for it bears testimony to the triumphant Christ.

Dead or alive? If Christ is dead, our faith is without foundation, but if he's alive, it means that Jesus is God, confirms that the Bible is true, and gives Christian faith a foundation that cannot be destroyed.

2. Forgiveness

The forgiveness of Christians depends on Jesus' resurrection. "If Christ has not been raised, your faith is futile; you are still in your sins." No resurrection, no forgiveness. You see, if Jesus was not raised, then God did not accept the death of Jesus as a sufficient sacrifice that paid for the sins of the world. If God didn't raise Jesus, then the death of that carpenter-turned-rabbi was just a sad case of a man getting himself killed and accomplishing nothing. This would mean that all people who count on Jesus to forgive and save them from sin are wrong.

But if God did raise Jesus, he was showing that he accepted Jesus' death as the sacrifice and final payment for sin and that he forgives everyone who belongs to Jesus. "He was delivered over to death for our sins and was raised to life for our justification" (Romans 4:25). God's forgiveness of Christians is real only if the risen body of Jesus is real.

Dead or alive? If Christ is dead, faith in him does not bring forgiveness, but if he's alive, then Jesus is the way to be forgiven from sin and made right with God—the only way.

3. Future

The future of Christians depends on Jesus' resurrection. If Christ has not been raised, Christians have no future. "Then those also who have fallen asleep in Christ are lost. If only for this life we have hope in Christ, we are to be pitied more than all men." Christians believe our bodies will be raised and will live forever because we believe Christ arose and lives forever. But if Christ didn't rise, then Christians won't rise. Once they die, they will stay dead, just like the mixed up teacher they believed in. If that's the case, Christians are the most self-deceived, pitiable fools around. Feel sorry for them if you like, but don't become one.

On the other hand, if Jesus has been raised in a glorified res- urrection body, then those who have gone to their graves trust- ing in him will also be raised to everlasting life. Death is not the end of the story. Life has conquered death, and the followers of Jesus can look forward to a splendid future. They will enjoy eternal life and joy and pleasures and blessings with their risen Savior. If Jesus is dead, Christians have a bleak future. If he's alive, they have a blessed future.

4. Fulfillment

The fulfillment of a Christian's purpose in life depends on the resurrection. Without it, life has no final meaning or purpose except to maximize our pleasure and minimize our pain. In Paul's words, "If I fought wild beasts in Ephesus for merely human reasons, what have I gained? If the dead are not raised, 'Let us eat and drink, for tomorrow we die'" (1 Corinthians 15:32). Why would anyone stand up for his beliefs, even to the point of being thrown to the lions, if death is the end? If there's nothing beyond death, then it's stupid to be a hero. Be a hedonist instead. Grab the gusto while you can. Have as much fun as you can before you become food for the worms. "Eat, drink, and be merry, for tomorrow you die." If death is the end, then there is no ultimate meaning to your life, and no final reckoning; God will never call you to account. If you're going to die like an animal, you might as well live like an animal, seeking pleasure and avoiding pain.

However, if Christ has been raised, then death is not the end, and each of us must stand before the judgment seat of Christ. Selfishness will be punished; self-sacrifice will be rewarded. Hedonism will turn out to be stupid, and heroism will turn out to be smart. Rejecting Christ will prove to be hell, and accepting Christ will turn out to be heaven.

Dead or alive? If Jesus is dead, then fulfillment is nothing more than doing whatever feels good for the moment, but if Jesus is alive, fulfillment is found in following Jesus, loving God, and loving others as he commands, even if it means pain and sacrifice at times.

Can you see why we can't afford to be fuzzy in our thinking about whether Jesus is dead or alive? We need to be clear and definite, because so much depends on it. The foundations of Christian teaching, the forgiveness of sins, the future destiny of Christians, and the fulfillment of our life's purpose all depend on whether Jesus is dead or alive. If he's dead, the only sensible choice is to forget him. If he's alive, the only sensible choice is to follow him.

Evidence for Jesus' Resurrection

The whole Christian faith depends on the belief that Jesus rose from the dead. So if you're wondering whether you should be a Christian, you need to make up your mind whether Jesus is dead or alive. Do you have to shut your brain off to believe in Jesus' resurrection? No, the Bible encourages us to look at the facts. Let's consider four kinds of evidence.

1. Old Testament Predictions

In 1 Corinthians 15, Paul writes "that Christ died for our sins *according to the Scriptures,* that he was buried, that he was raised on the third day *according to the Scriptures.*"

In the books of the Old Testament, written centuries before Jesus was born, we find many prophecies about the Messiah. The prophets predicted the Messiah would be born in Bethlehem. They predicted his ministry would shine in Galilee. They predicted he would enter Jerusalem riding a donkey. They predicted the Messiah would be betrayed by a friend, beaten and spit on and pierced by his enemies, his clothes divided by gambling. They predicted he would die and be buried in a borrowed grave. All these things happened to Jesus. Just a coincidence? Not likely. If all the predictions about the Messiah fit one particular man, then that man has to be the Messiah. And if Jesus is the Messiah who fulfills so many Old Testament prophecies, isn't it reasonable to expect that he would also fulfill Old Testament prophecies predicting his resurrection?

For instance, consider Isaiah 53. Writing long before the time of Jesus, Isaiah spoke of how God's servant would die for the sins of his people. But the prophet went on to say, "After the suffering of his soul, *he will see the light of life* and be satisfied" (53:11). Or look at Psalm 16:10, which says, "You will not abandon me to the grave, nor will you let your Holy One see decay." Jesus' resurrection would fulfill those prophecies and others like them.

Ancient prophecy is one strong reason to believe Jesus is alive, but it's not the only one. In fact, if prophecy had been the only evidence, it's unlikely that the early Christians would have believed in Jesus' resurrection. As the apostle John put it, "They still did not understand from Scripture that Jesus had to rise from the dead" (John 20:9). But they had other evidence.

2. *The Empty Tomb*

John tells us that what first convinced him of the resurrection was the empty tomb. On the first Easter, John went to the tomb and saw with his own eyes that the body was gone. He saw the strips of linen and the burial cloth that had been wrapped around Jesus' head still lying there, but Jesus himself was nowhere to be found. John saw this, and he believed (John 20:3-9).

This is exhibit #2 in the evidence that the resurrection really happened: the empty tomb. There's no denying that Jesus' body was gone. Otherwise, when the disciples started saying Jesus was alive, the government officials and religious authorities would have produced the body to show that he was still dead. But Jesus' body had disappeared.

And it wasn't easy to explain how. Some of Jesus' enemies spread a rumor that his disciples had come and stolen the body in an attempt to fool people into believing that Jesus was alive. But how likely is that? The disciples were shattered by Jesus' death. They were in no mood to pull a practical joke and try to fool anyone. Besides, there was a squad of heavily armed soldiers guarding Jesus' tomb. How could a few heartbroken fishermen sneak past professional troops?

And what did they have to gain by stealing the body and preaching Jesus' resurrection? This wasn't some swindle where they all got rich. A politician might lie to stay in power, a salesman might lie to make money, but what did Jesus' followers have to gain by lying about seeing him alive? All they got out of it was persecution, prison, torture, and death. All of the apostles were either martyred or exiled, so it's nonsense to explain the empty tomb by saying the disciples stole the body and then lied about the resurrection because they had something to gain by it. No, the only explanation that makes any sense of the empty tomb is that Jesus actually came back to life. And the only thing that explains why Jesus' disciples were willing to die rather than change their story is that they were telling the truth when they said they had seen Jesus alive. That brings us to the third type of evidence for the resurrection: the eyewitness testimony.

3. Eyewitness Testimony

In 1 Corinthians 15 Paul writes that Jesus "appeared to Peter, and then to the Twelve. After that, he appeared to more than five hundred of the brothers at the same time, most of whom are still living, though some have fallen asleep. Then he appeared to James, then to all the apostles, and last of all he appeared to me, as to one abnormally born."

The living Lord appeared to many people, and these weren't just mysterious visions. No, Jesus actually spoke with his followers, he broke bread with them, he ate fish with them, he even invited Thomas, the most skeptical of the disciples, to touch his scars. When he appeared to some women, they fell before him and actually held on to his feet and worshipped him. Not only that, but on some occasions, he appeared to large groups who all saw and heard him at the same time. They couldn't all be dreaming or hallucinating at the same time.

Now, if you were part of a jury, and you had the testimony of hundreds of reliable, level-headed people who all said they saw a certain person—and those people were willing to die rather than change their story—wouldn't you believe them?

4. Changed Lives

A fourth kind of evidence for Jesus' resurrection is also convincing: the change that Jesus makes in people's lives. Paul points to himself as a prime example. He says, "For I am the least of the apostles and do not even deserve to be called an apostle, because I persecuted the church of God. But by the grace of God, I am what I am, and his grace to me was not without effect" (1 Corinthians 15:9-10).

Jesus didn't just appear to Paul; he changed him. Paul was once a proud, self-righteous man who imprisoned and killed Christians. But the living Christ transformed Paul into a kind, loving man who became the greatest missionary who ever lived.

Paul wasn't the only person Jesus changed. When Jesus was about to go on trial, his friend Peter behaved like a coward and denied knowing Jesus. But after seeing the risen Lord, Peter changed into a courageous preacher. Jesus' half-brother James, along with the rest of his relatives, had once thought Jesus was out of his mind. But when Jesus appeared to his brothers after his resurrection, they believed in him and changed into different people. Jesus changes those who trust him.

That's been true throughout the history of the Christian church, and it's still true today. Physically, Christ has remained in heaven since his ascension, but by the written testimony of his apostles and by the power of his Spirit, Jesus continues to convince people that he is real, and he changes their lives. Millions of people from all nations, young and old, rich and poor, uneducated and geniuses, have been changed by Christ. They're not only convinced Jesus is alive; they love him and have a vital relationship with him.

When you put the evidence together—the Old Testament predictions, the empty tomb, the hundreds of eyewitnesses, and the millions of people whose lives Christ has changed—it makes good sense to believe in the resurrection. It makes good sense to say with Paul, "Christ has indeed been raised from the dead!" It makes good sense to become a Christian, to put your faith in Jesus as the risen Lord and the eternal Son of God.

Making the Leap

Ultimately, it's not enough simply to weigh the evidence and believe a historical fact. Once you conclude that Jesus is alive, the consequences are enormous. As we saw earlier, your foundation, your forgiveness, your future, your fulfillment all are found in the living Christ. So trust in the Lord Jesus as the Son of God, and believe the Bible as the Word of God. Ask God to forgive you for the sake of Jesus' death on the cross, and trust that he will do so. Rejoice that the eternal life of Jesus can be yours as well. Then pursue the purpose of your life by obeying the risen Lord and going wherever he leads, no matter what it costs you.

Are you still hesitating? Maybe you want all your questions answered and all your doubts resolved before you give up on yourself and give in to Jesus. You want to know why God allows problems and tragedies. You want answers to every last question about Bible passages that seem difficult. You want ironclad proof of resurrection and life after death. You want proof positive that Jesus is real. You want to be 100 percent sure before you risk putting your life in his hands. But if you're waiting for all risk and uncertainty to go away, you won't come to Jesus at all.

Faith involves risking your life, betting everything you have on the power of Jesus Christ and the reality of resurrection. You can't be saved by playing it safe. "For whoever wants to save his life will lose it," says Jesus, "but whoever loses his life for me will find it" (Matthew 16:25).

When I talk about risk, I'm not saying there aren't sound reasons for becoming a Christian. As we've seen, there are strong reasons to believe that God is real and that he controls this world. There are strong reasons to believe that the Bible is reliable. There are strong reasons to believe that Jesus rose from the dead. Rational study shows that Christianity is reasonable, even probable, but we still might not feel sure, given the way our minds tend to operate.

Not only does rational study show strong probability, it also shows us what is at stake in the decision to follow Jesus. As the philosopher Pascal pointed out, if you bet on resurrection and win, you win everything; if you lose, you lose nothing you wouldn't have lost anyway. If you bet on resurrection and you're right, you win forgiveness, joy, and eternal life, and you also become a better, more loving person in this life. If you bet against resurrection and you're wrong, you lose everything. You live on a lower level in this life, and in the life to come you lose the happiness of heaven and condemn yourself to the aloneness and suffering of hell as the final result of your self-centered life. Logical reasoning can't remove every doubt about resurrection, and it can't make your decision for you, but it does show the evidence for resurrection, and it shows that you have everything to gain and little to lose by risking your life on Jesus.

Philosopher Peter Kreeft compares it to standing at the window of a burning building. A rescue team moves in with a safety net to a position directly below you. They call out to you, "Jump! We'll catch you." However, the smoke is thick around you, stinging your eyes and making them watery. You shout back, "I can't see you. What if I jump and you don't catch me?" They shout back, "You can't see us, but we see you. We're in the right spot. Trust us!" At that point, you have two options. You can just keep standing there, wishing you could see more clearly—and you will burn. Or you can trust the voices calling to you, and you can jump. Only when you land do you know for sure that throwing your life into their hands was really safe.

So, too, faith seems like a big risk when the smoke of this world gets in your eyes and keeps you from seeing clearly. But the living Lord Jesus is absolutely real, and he catches every person who takes the leap of faith. Faith might seem like a risk from where you're standing, but that doesn't mean it's not certain. It just means you won't feel the certainty until you take that leap of faith and land in the arms of Jesus. Then, as Pascal put it, "you will gain even in this life... and you will see that your gain is so certain and your risk so negligible that in the end you will realize that you have wagered on something certain and infinite for which you have paid nothing."

Chapter 10

Resurrection and Other Religions

Are all religions equally true and equally helpful in bringing people to the ultimate good? Or is faith in Jesus unique and able to do what no other religion can do? Looking at Jesus' resurrection, we see some ways that Christianity is decisively different from other religions.

Leader Like No Other

Jesus' resurrection shows who he is: the eternal Son of God in human flesh. The Bible says Jesus was "declared with power to be the Son of God by his resurrection from the dead" (Romans 1:4). When Jesus' disciple Thomas saw the risen Christ, he worshipped him, saying, "My Lord and my God" (John 20:28). In defeating death and showing his deity, Jesus stands apart from the leaders of other world religions.

The risen Jesus stands apart from Muhammad, the founder of Islam. Muhammad's preaching and military power conquered Arabia before his death in the year 632. Muhammad's body did not rise from the dead; he did not show himself to his friends after his death. Muhammad never claimed to be divine and never allowed anyone to worship him. Indeed, Muhammad's book, the Koran, says it's grievous to say God has a son. Muhammad considered Jesus a prophet but insisted that nobody could be the Son of God. The Koran threatens punishment and hell for those who say Jesus is God come to earth. How can all religions be true if the Christian view of Jesus is considered blasphemy by Muslims? Somebody must be wrong on this vital point. Muhammad rejected anything in the Bible that differed from his own teaching, despite the fact that Muhammad lived 600 years after Jesus. The New Testament gospels were written by personal friends of Jesus who knew him well. They heard him claim equality with God, saw him die, saw him alive and victorious over death, and worshiped him as Lord and God. Jesus accepted their worship, something Muhammad would never have done.

The risen Jesus stands apart from Confucius, another major figure in world religion. Confucius was a smart man who made a major impact on the behavior and beliefs of millions, especially in China. But when Confucius died at age 73, his body remained dead. After his death, some people began to revere and worship him. Worshipping and praying to dead ancestors was common among the Chinese, and the dead Confucius became a leading object of devotion. But Confucius never claimed to be divine. He gave advice on how to deal with other people, much of it quite sensible. He also admitted that he did not live up to his own standards. Unlike Confucius, Jesus said he lived perfectly, without any fault. Unlike Confucius, Jesus spoke of being on a level with God (John 8:46-58). And Jesus' claims were shown to be true when he rose from the dead.

The risen Jesus stands apart from the Buddha. The Buddha lived over eighty years and then died. The Buddha's body did not rise from the dead, and he never said he would rise. Unlike Jesus, the Buddha never claimed to be God. He didn't even believe in a personal God but in an impersonal nirvana. Jesus, on the other hand, spoke of a loving heavenly Father, spoke of himself as the Father's eternal Son, and rose again to prove it.

The risen Jesus stands apart from Hinduism and other Eastern religions related to it. There are many forms of Hinduism, but most Hindus recognize various gods and goddesses. They believe that "all gods and goddesses are but various aspects of the one Absolute *Brahman*," the vast force that pervades all things. What's more, they believe each human and every other form of life has God within. To find God you simply look inside yourself. In Hinduism the ultimate goal is to escape your bodily existence, get out of the cycle of one reincarnation after another, stop being a distinct person, and merge your consciousness with the God-force, *Brahman*. All things are one with God, whether they realize it or not, so it's no big deal to say Jesus is God. Isn't everybody? Some Hindus give Jesus a special place as an avatar, one of a number of incarnations of the God-Force that have been especially effective in helping others to find the God within. This Hindu view clashes with Christianity. Jesus, in rising from the dead, turns out to be different from any avatar or guru. Jesus is unique. He is the one and only person who is truly God incarnate in human form. If we want to find God, we must seek him in Jesus, not in ourselves or in anything else.

Jesus' resurrection demonstrates his deity and sets him apart from the leading figures of every other religion. Only Jesus claimed to be God's only Son. Only Jesus established his claim by dying and coming back to life in an immortal body. The risen Christ himself said, "I am the First and the Last. I am the Living One; I was dead, and behold I am alive forever and ever! And I hold the keys of death and Hades" (Revelation 1:17-18).

Our Greatest Need

As Jesus' resurrection shows the difference between the Son of God and the founders of other religions, it also shows that our greatest need is different from what other religions say we need most. Our greatest need is for someone to save us from our sin and give us victory over death. Jesus' death is the only sufficient payment for the sins of the world, and his resurrection brings victory over death and unending enjoyment of a new creation in fellowship with God. Again, this sets Christianity apart from other world religions.

According to Hinduism, the problem is not that we've offended a holy and personal God who rules over us. The problem is that we haven't yet discovered the impersonal God-force who is already inside us. The Hindu goal is not physical resurrection and eternal life as a person with a distinct identity enjoying fellowship with a personal God. The goal is to escape the physical world completely and lose your identity by merging into the

vast, impersonal oneness of Brahman. The way to do this is
through meditation and continual effort. You go through as
many lives and reincarnations as it takes until you achieve this.

Buddhism, which began as an offshoot of Hinduism and has
much in common with it, takes a similar approach. According to
Buddhism, humanity's biggest problem is lack of awareness, and
what you need most is to give up all desire, achieve release from
physical existence and personal identity, and lose yourself in nirvana. You must achieve this entirely through your own efforts.
Theravada Buddhists have a saying:

No one saves us but ourselves,

No one can and no one may;

We ourselves must tread the Path:

Buddhas only show the way.

The Buddha told his followers not to count on any god or
gods to help them but only on themselves: "Those who, relying
upon themselves only, shall not look for assistance to anyone besides themselves, it is they who shall reach the topmost height."
In contrast, Jesus says, "Apart from me you can do nothing"
(John 15:5). You can't pay for sin or conquer death on your
own. You cannot rely on yourself only; you must depend totally
on God.

Hinduism, Buddhism, and related religions tend to be pantheistic, teaching that all is God and God is all. The physical
world turns out to be unreal, and individual identity turns out to
be an illusion. Indeed, the view that all is God means that there
is no real distinction between God and other beings, no real distinction between good and evil, light and darkness, life and
death. This idea appears at a popular level in the *Star Wars* films:
the Force has a good side and a dark side, but both sides are part
of the same universal Force. This is like the yin/yang of Taoism:
opposites turn out not to be opposites after all.

But according to Jesus, sin is not one with holiness, and
death is not one with life. Sin is bad. Death is an enemy. Our
great problem is that we are sinners doomed to die, and we can't
change our predicament. But Jesus can, and he has. To deal with

sin, Jesus lived a perfect life, gave himself as a sacrifice to pay the penalty of sin, and credits his perfection to those who rely on him. To deal with death, Jesus entered into it, overcame it by the power of God, and rose to life in a glorified, immortal body. It is by faith in his blood and his victory over death, not through our own achievements, that we enter eternal life. Jesus' resurrection marks Christianity as utterly different from pantheistic religions that deny the seriousness of sin, the tragedy of death, and the joy of having an immortal body and belonging forever to a personal and holy God.

Islam and Judaism differ from pantheist religions and are closer to Christianity in some important ways. There is belief in a personal Creator and creatures who are distinct from the Lord, and there is also an awareness that sin offends God, that death is a bad thing, and that personal, bodily existence is a good thing. But Islam and Judaism refuse to recognize Jesus as the Son of God and reject the crucified and risen Christ as the source of forgiveness and eternal life. Despite some common ground between Islam, Judaism, and Christianity, the resurrection of Jesus represents a great difference and a parting of the ways.

Jesus and his early followers were Jewish, and some Jewish people today believe in Jesus as the Messiah promised in the Hebrew Scripture. But the religious institutions of Judaism insist that faith in Jesus means the abandonment, not the fulfillment, of Jewishness. Some branches of Judaism largely ignore life after death, while other branches teach that a person's destiny depends on one's own level of righteousness, not on God's grace in Jesus the Messiah.

Islam likewise bases eternal life on earning it, not on faith in Jesus as Savior. Muslims don't believe the resurrection happened because they don't believe Jesus died on the cross at all. They believe someone else, probably Judas, was made to look like Jesus and was nailed to the cross instead of Jesus. The enemies of Jesus thought they killed him, but they actually killed someone else. God fooled them. Jesus himself was taken directly to heaven without dying. In Muslim thinking, sin is not covered by Jesus' blood, and death is not defeated by Jesus' resurrection. Islam teaches that people are saved by being good enough. Islam denies that all humanity is fallen and born into the powerful grip of sin. According to Muslim teaching, all people are born good but forgetful; they just need to be reminded of what God wants. Humans don't need salvation—they just need the guidance of Islamic law on what they must do to meet the requirements for getting into heaven. Islam is a religion of rules: the best thing God has done for us is giving a law that tells us exactly what to do. Christianity is a religion of love: the best thing God has done for us is giving himself in the person of Jesus to die and rise again for our salvation.

There is no way to avoid or minimize the difference between faith in the risen Jesus and all other religions. Only Jesus' atoning death meets our need to be rescued from the guilt and grip of sin, and only Jesus' resurrection defeats death and provides eternal life. Christ Jesus "has destroyed death and has brought life and immortality to light through the gospel" (2 Timothy 1:10).

The Appointed Judge

Another major difference between resurrection faith and other world religions has to do with the final judgment. Judgment Day is coming, and the Judge won't be Krishna or Confucius or Muhammad or the Buddha or the Dalai Lama. The Judge will be Jesus. The Bible says God "has set a day when he will judge the world with justice by the man he has appointed. He has given proof of this to all men by raising him from the dead" (Acts 17:31). Nobody will be exempt from appearing before Jesus. "He will judge *the world*," people of every place and background. In Jesus' resurrection, God provides proof "to *all* people" of who will be their Judge (and who won't be).

The resurrection also shows the nature of the final judgment. Your future is not many reincarnations in various bodies. Your future is exactly one resurrection in an immortal body. You will not merge with an impersonal force called Brahman or nirvana. You will stand before a Judge named Jesus, and he will either welcome you to the joy of God's new heaven and earth or else banish you to the misery of hell. "Multitudes who sleep in the dust of the earth will awake: some to everlasting life, others to shame and everlasting contempt" (Daniel 12:2). You only live once; you only die once; you only are resurrected and judged once (Hebrews 9:27-28). You must be ready to face the Judge when the time comes. His judgment is final. After that there will be no second chances. Your future will be fixed: everlasting life or everlasting contempt.

If Jesus will preside as Judge and we can be saved only through faith in him, does that mean non-Christian religions are wrong about everything? No, various religions may contain important insights. They may know something of the human hunger for a spiritual dimension and offer moral guidelines on how to treat each other. Most religions are right about some things, but only biblical faith is right about the things that matter most: recognizing Jesus as God with us, dealing with sin and defeating death, and making us ready to stand before the Judge. Jesus is not just one among many paths to God; Jesus is the only Way. "Whoever believes in him is not condemned, but whoever does not believe in him stands condemned already because he has not believed in the name of God's one and only Son" (John 3:18).

Some traditions assume humanity is basically good and then offer advice on how to become even better. In the tradition of Confucius, for example, the first sentence millions of children have learned to read is, "Human beings are by nature good." With guidance and tradition, good humans become better. Islam takes a similar approach. A leading Muslim scholar says, "The Christian belief in the redemptive sacrificial death of Christ does not fit the Islamic view that man has always been fundamentally good." However, if you assume you're good by nature, you will never be ready to face Jesus the Judge. You are a sinner. Your sins are not just occasional mistakes; your sins arise from a sinful nature that you can't conquer just by advice and traditions.

"You must be born again," says Jesus (John 3:7). You must receive a new nature through faith in Christ and have his Holy

Spirit take charge of your life. The gospel of Christ is not just a nice person telling nice people how to be a bit nicer. The gospel is God's power to save sinful people headed for hell, make them new, and bring them to heaven. The gospel tells you how to get ready to face Jesus the Judge and rejoice to see him. That brings us to a final difference between faith in Jesus' resurrection and all other world religions: our eternal destiny.

Final Destiny

If you believe in the risen Jesus, you know that the final destiny of the Lord's people is personal and physical. Some religions teach a final future where people leave their physical bodies behind forever, escaping the world of matter into the realm of pure spirit. Even their spirits don't remain individual and personal but are absorbed into one vast, impersonal God-force. But Jesus' resurrection contradicts such ideas. When the risen Jesus appeared to his disciples, he was still the same person they had known, and his body remained real. "It is I myself!" Jesus said. "Touch me and see; a ghost does not have flesh and bones, as you see I have" (Luke 24:39).

Since Jesus rose bodily and continues in his body for eternity, we may be sure that our bodies and the physical world are part of the splendid new creation that awaits us. The intellectual and spiritual joys will be great, but the physical dimension will also be wonderful. The physical creation around us is not headed for ruin but for renewal. Our bodies are not burdens to be trashed but blessings to be treasured and eventually transformed. Jesus "will transform our lowly bodies so that they will be like his glorious body" (Philippians 3:21). Biblical faith declares, "I know that my Redeemer lives, and that in the end he will stand upon the earth. And after my skin has been destroyed, yet in my flesh I will see God" (Job 19:25-26).

So don't believe any teaching which says the human body or the physical world doesn't belong in the ultimate future. Matter matters. Jesus' resurrection means that bodies are forever. Don't believe anyone who says the ultimate good is to escape personal, individual existence and be swallowed up in a universal, impersonal power. The ultimate good is to know the personal love of God in Christ and to experience his resurrection power and life. One of Jesus' early followers said, "I consider everything a loss compared to the surpassing greatness of knowing Christ Jesus my Lord...I want to know Christ and the power of his resurrection" (Philippians 3:8-10). Already on earth we aim to know Christ better, and when we see our Lord face to face, our joy will be complete. We will have the personal identity God created us to have; Jesus will be the same person he has always been; and we will enjoy unending friendship with the Lord and with all his people.

Are you beginning to grasp how faith in the risen Jesus differs from all other religions? At first it may sound open-minded to say all religions are equally true, but it turns out to be nonsense. The differences are too great. If you've been confused by the variety of religion options, it's time to cut through the confusion. Zero in on just one thing: the resurrection of Jesus. If there were no resurrection, if Jesus remained dead, then the Christian faith would be false and empty. You could then forget about Christianity and either be an atheist or pursue another religion. But Jesus did rise again, and he's very much alive. Accept him as the way, the truth, and the life. There is no other.

Chapter 11

Craving Atonement

School kids can be like Aztecs.

Centuries ago the Aztecs ruled an empire in the area that is now Mexico. The Aztecs had a clever, advanced culture in some ways, but human sacrifice was a standard part of life. The Aztecs went to war on a regular basis to seize thousands of people as sacrifices for their gods. The Aztecs would take the captives to the top of a temple pyramid and torture them over a fire until their skin was blistered with burns. Then the priests would pull the victims away from the fire, still alive and in agony. The priests would lay each victim on a large stone block, cut open the chest, and rip out the beating heart. As one historian describes it, this was "a messy affair, with priests, stone, platform and steps all drenched by the spurting blood. The head of the victim was usually severed and spitted on a skull rack while the lifeless body was pushed and rolled down the pyramid steps. At the base of the pyramid, the body was butchered and, after being distributed to relatives and friends of the warrior who had offered the sacrifice, the parts were cooked and eaten." Sometimes a sauce of peppers and tomatoes was added for extra flavor.

It's awful to think such things really happened, and it may seem outrageous to compare school kids to Aztecs. But kids can be as eager as Aztecs to seek out victims, torment them, rip out their heart, and swallow them up. Some kids feel a need to pick on other kids until the victims are destroyed. Gang members and youthful thugs can be cruel, and they're not the only ones. Even respectable students and star athletes can be involved in making life miserable for designated victims. Gangs use physical cruelty, but there are other, non-physical ways to torture a person, tear out her heart, and destroy her identity. Human sacrifice of the spirit happens when kids make others miserable. Cannibalism of the spirit happens when they nourish their own sense of self at the expense of others. Countless school-age boys and girls suffer mockery, rejection, and cruelty. The life and joy are drained out of them.

Why would kids be so cruel? Well, it seems to come naturally. Some unrealistic intellectuals have said children are born innocent and tribal peoples are noble. But the opposite appears to be true. Children and tribal peoples tend to be as cruel as anyone. From an early age, most kids have a mean streak. Even small toddlers bite, pull hair, and hit others. Brothers and sisters say and do things to hurt each other and to make each other look bad. Schoolmates target certain kids for constant, merciless taunting and torment.

Whatever it is that makes kids cruel, they aren't just cruel to others. Often kids are cruel to themselves too. Many young people are mysteriously drawn to pain and self-destructive behavior. Some start smoking, fully aware that it harms them. Some use drugs and drink alcohol with almost suicidal determination. Some become sexually promiscuous, bringing on themselves degradation, heartbreak, and disease. Some drift into self-destructive eating disorders, such as anorexia—and the fact that anorexia can harm or even kill is part of the attraction.

Some submit themselves to painful tattooing, piercing, and body modification, relishing pain and disfigurement. Some young people cut themselves and say that watching themselves bleed makes them feel better. A 14-year-old boy said he wanted to pierce his tongue, nose, and more private parts. Asked about the reason, he said, "I don't really know why. In the past I have found that by inflicting pain on myself I could release a lot of anger and emotion without hurting anyone else. For about 4 months I would say that I was addicted to pain, I would slash my arms with a razor or a knife every time I became angry." He was driven by a need to suffer.

Kids also hurt and sacrifice themselves in less physical ways. The headmaster of a private school writes about bright students who manage to fail classes. The students are gifted enough and the classes are easy enough that the students could get good grades with what they absorb in the classroom, with no study at all. But they still fail. They couldn't fail unless they wanted to— but apparently failure is what they want. The headmaster views this as a form of self-punishment. The students have the talent to succeed, but something tells them they don't *deserve* success, so they plunge farther and farther into failure. Pain has such a pull on some kids that they would rather fail than flourish.

Individuals Craving Atonement

What causes cruelty to self and cruelty to others? At the heart of much cruelty lies a deep sense of unworthiness. This unworthiness, this guilt, might not be consciously recognized or put into words by those affected, but it controls them anyway. When someone sins, someone must pay. Someone must atone by suffering. Either I must suffer or someone else must suffer, but somehow there must be suffering. There must be payment through pain. There must be atonement. This craving for atonement drives sadism (savoring the pain of others) and masochism (seeking pain for oneself). This affects not just ancient civilizations or confused kids but grownups as well.

Atonement is a deep and basic need, and only God can meet this need. He provides atonement through the suffering and death of Jesus Christ. "God presented him as a sacrifice of atonement through faith in his blood" (Romans 3:25). "He is the atoning sacrifice for our sins, and not only for ours but also for the sins of the whole world" (1 John 2:2). "He himself bore our sins in his body on the tree" (1 Peter 2:24), the cross where Jesus suffered and died. Those who trust Christ's atonement are freed from the craving for atonement that drives them to inflict pain on others or on themselves. Jesus has already paid the price.

But those who don't know forgiveness and freedom in Christ's atonement are driven to seek atonement in some other way, by victimizing others, by becoming victims themselves, or by doing both. Even if theorists and therapists try to make us feel good about ourselves, even if we don't admit our guilt and don't have a conscious terror of God's punishment, our fear and guilt and craving for atonement still come out, often in the ways we inflict pain on ourselves and others.

We've talked about the cruelty of ancient Aztecs and modern youth, but what about the adults among us? Many married people mistreat and abuse their spouses and children. Abuse among unmarried live-ins is even worse. Why be so cruel to the people closest to us? The craving for atonement is a major factor. Abusers often project their guilt onto others and then punish them painfully. However, the suffering of others cannot satisfy the abusers' craving for atonement. Meanwhile, an astonishing number of abused spouses and live-ins continue to take a beating. For some reason, they can't bring themselves to leave their abusers behind. And if they do leave the abuser behind and seek a new relationship, they often seem to have a magnet that draws them to another abuser. Why is this? Perhaps it's because they are using their own suffering and victimhood as a way to satisfy their craving for atonement.

Another form of self-punishment occurs among drunkards and drug users. Many addicts have a gnawing sense of unworthiness and a craving for atonement. Something inside says they don't deserve to be healthy and happy but deserve pain and misery. Drinking and drugging oneself into a miserable life and an early grave becomes a misguided way to pay for sin. This craving for atonement dominates not only addicted people but also people who are drawn to addicts. Why do so many people who grew up miserable with an alcoholic parent end up marrying an alcoholic and continuing in misery? Why do people with alcoholic spouses stick with them and suffer unbearable things and cover for them? And why, if people break up with addicted spouses or live-in lovers, do they so often end up with another partner who is as addicted and messed up as the previous one? Victimhood attracts many people like an invisible magnet. They're driven by unworthiness and a craving to suffer and atone for their loved ones and themselves.

Some people simply can't bear to be treated well and to enjoy life. If they get a steady job with good pay, they soon provoke a showdown with their boss that gets them fired. If they have enough money to make ends meet, they gamble or chase foolish financial schemes till they're deep in debt. If their spouse is kind and faithful, they provoke their spouse almost as if they want the spouse to be cruel or adulterous. Such people *need* a crisis. They *need* things to go wrong for them. They *need* to punish themselves and at the same time blame someone else. They can't live with a normal, pleasant situation. They might not know what drives them, but the truth is that they crave pain and victimhood in order to atone for their unworthiness.

When people aren't cruel to others or to themselves in everyday life, they still may wallow in pain by plunging into entertainment that focuses on suffering. They watch soap operas with one sad story after another. They listen to music about abuse, torture, and shattered relationships. They watch movies about serial killers, cannibals, blood-sucking vampires, and monsters. They are drawn to blood and pain. Something in them relishes the suffering of others and relishes their own horror.

The urge to make someone suffer, or to make yourself suffer, can produce dreadful results. A pregnant woman found out that her husband had an affair with another woman. She was terribly upset. She didn't divorce him, but she was furious at him and wanted to make him suffer for his unfaithfulness. Her husband was eager for a baby, so she decided to abort their baby in order to punish her husband for his betrayal. Afterward, though, she felt worse about the abortion than she had felt about her husband's adultery. The baby's death was her choice, not his; the guilt of the abortion was hers, not his. So how did she respond? When she got pregnant again, she aborted the second baby too! She explained, "I wanted to be able to hate myself more for what I did to the first baby." Her guilty conscience and craving for atonement drove her to keep adding to her sin and suffering.

The ways individuals harm others and themselves are twisted and sad, but at the root of such warped things is something valid: the need for atonement. When somebody sins, somebody pays. Unless we count on the payment made by Christ, our craving for atonement will not be satisfied, and we will seek relief by inflicting pain on others or by plunging into pain ourselves. This is what happens when we don't rest in the real atonement God provides by the sacrifice of Jesus on the cross.

Cultures Craving Atonement

The craving for atonement drives not only individuals but entire cultures. It's no accident that many societies and religions without Christ have practiced ritual human sacrifice or other public spectacles of suffering and slaughter. Throughout history these horrors have been committed on a massive scale in many different parts of the world.

In Central America, the Aztecs and the Mayans had the two most prominent cultures, and both Aztecs and Mayans sacrificed prisoners of war and butchered countless children. In South America, the Incas of Peru offered child sacrifices, and the Tupi of Brazil were cannibals. In North America tribes such as the Pawnee, Natchez, Iroquois, Anasazi, and Huron—to name just a few—had similar customs. For example, according to a noted historian using eyewitness accounts, Hurons would take a man from a rival tribe, and they would take turns burning the captive's skin in different places. They would spend all night pressing red-hot hatchets and poking burning sticks into various body parts. Then they would gouge out his eyes, cut off his hands and feet with the victim still alive, cut off his head, and roast him for a meal. (I hate to describe such things, and believe it or not, I've left out the most sickening details.) African tribes and islanders of the Pacific also practiced human sacrifice and cannibalism.

The Middle East and Mediterranean world also had human sacrifice. The mighty civilization of Carthage sought success by sacrificing babies to its pagan gods. Before the Old Testament Israelites conquered Canaan, the pagan Canaanites tried to please their gods and goddesses by sacrificing their own children. Nations bordering Israel continued with horrible cruelty and human sacrifice, and there were times even in Israel and Judah when kings knew of the true God but turned away from him to other religions and burned their own children (2 Kings 16:3, 21:6). The people did the same, sacrificing "their sons and daughters in the fire" (Jeremiah 7:31).

Most of us, if we could trace our roots back far enough, would find people in our family tree who were involved in human sacrifice. In Europe, Germanic tribes practiced human sacrifice until faith in Christ triumphed over paganism. Irish tribes sacrificed babies to their harvest gods and sacrificed prisoners of war to their war gods. They stopped only after St. Patrick brought the gospel to the Irish. Italians filled the stadiums of Rome to enjoy one bloodbath after another, slaughtering captives from other nations, forcing gladiators to fight each other. When Christianity began to spread, Roman emperors blamed Christians for anything that went wrong in the Roman empire and killed them in all sorts of horrible ways. But Christianity kept spreading, and eventually the killing in the stadiums ended.

In more recent times, human sacrifice has been less common as a religious ritual, thanks to the spread of Christianity. But anti-Christian ideologies have found other ways to blame and sacrifice people. The French revolution was anti-God and slaughtered countless people as a bloody sacrifice to produce a new and glorious society—which turned out to be nothing but a reign of terror. Hitler and the Nazis blamed Germany's problems on the Jews and slaughtered millions as a human sacrifice to produce a thousand-year Reich for the master race. Lenin and Stalin blamed Christians and capitalists for all of Russia's woes and murdered millions in an effort to buy a new paradise with their blood. Mao blamed China's problems on everyone with any ability or property and wiped out millions of them. Pol Pot did the same in Cambodia.

These tyrants and terrorists were people who rejected Christ's atonement for sin, made someone else a scapegoat for their own evil, and then killed with bloody abandon. A case of this in our own time is Islamist extremism. Denying their own sinful nature and rejecting Christ's atonement, militant Muslims have an unsatisfied inner craving for atonement. They need to blame somebody and sacrifice somebody to pay for what's wrong with their society. They may blame the Jews, they may blame America, they may blame some of their own leaders, but they've got to blame *somebody* and make them suffer. These terrorists plunge into murder and suicide with wild abandon, thinking that such bloodshed pleases their god and opens the way to a new and better world. This is just one more example which shows that when Christ's atonement is not accepted, the social and political consequences can be severe.

Real Atonement

The suffering and death of Jesus on a cross is not just a long-ago, faraway event. Atonement through Jesus' blood is not just a weird, primitive doctrine with no relevance for today's world. We've seen that faith in real atonement, or lack of it, has enormous personal and political consequences. Atonement through Jesus' blood is the only way for individuals to have their guilt canceled, their deep craving for atonement satisfied, and thus to be free of the need to inflict pain on self and others. Atonement through Jesus' blood is also a life-giving source of political freedom and sanity. The gospel of Christ crucified and risen brought an end to human sacrifice in one society after another throughout history, and still today faith in Christ's atonement protects against guilt, resentment, and class warfare, things that mark a craving for atonement and spawn tyranny and terrorism.

Inside every one of us, and at the heart of entire societies, is a terrible secret. We are all sinners at heart, guilty before God and unworthy of happiness. Something deep inside senses that we must suffer and bleed or that someone else must suffer and bleed. We feel that something must change and that change must come through suffering. And it's true: we do deserve to bleed, and change can come only if someone suffers.

But the answer is not to bring pain on ourselves or to project our guilt onto others and heap cruelty on them. That's the ungodly attempt at atonement. God's answer to our need for atonement is the blood of Jesus Christ. He was pierced for our sins (Isaiah 53:5). Jesus' blood poured out on the cross has the power to do what our own bleeding cannot do. His blood washes away sin and cleanses the conscience as nothing else can.

You might think sin isn't all that serious or that it's not necessary to have blood atonement in order for sins to be forgiven. But God says otherwise. The Bible shows that there's a law built into the very structure of the universe: when somebody sins, somebody pays. There is no such thing as a sin that is simply overlooked or forgotten. All sin has to be dealt with. That's the way God has structured reality. When somebody sins, somebody must pay, and the payment must be suffering and death. Nothing can change that fundamental law of the universe. It is as certain as the law of gravity.

Every sin must be paid for, either with the life of the sinner or with the life of a substitute. We've discussed many ways people harm themselves and are cruel to others, driven by the unsatisfied craving to atone for their guilt. But no sinner can pay the full penalty for his own sin, and no sinner can substitute for another as payment for sin. Only someone who is without sin and deserves no punishment can be a suitable substitute for another.

As a perfect man, Jesus could take the place of other humans, and as the Son of God, he had the power to bear all the sins of the world. The Bible says Jesus "loved us and gave himself up for us as a fragrant offering and sacrifice to God" (Ephesians 5:2). It wasn't nails that kept Jesus on the cross; it was love that kept him there, as he provided the atonement we need in order to be forgiven and accepted by God.

Transferring Responsibility

On the cross Jesus took the responsibility for human sin, and he took the punishment for it. "God made him who had no sin to be sin for us" (2 Corinthians 5:21). You might wonder, "How can one person take responsibility for someone else and suffer the penalty they deserve? How can responsibility be transferred from us to Jesus?" We will never understand fully how God did this, but here are examples that might at least give us a hint.

One example is corporate responsibility. Suppose a big company buys a small business which is in financial trouble. As soon as the big company takes ownership, it becomes responsible for the business it purchased. The past debts have to be paid off, and any problems that this newly purchased business may have in the future will also be the responsibility of the company that bought it. One entity takes responsibility for the other, including all of its liabilities; that's part of the deal when a purchase is made.

Jesus bought us with a price (1 Corinthians 6:20). One aspect of that purchase is that he takes responsibility for all of our debts and problems and sins. By choosing to buy us and take ownership of us, he has made our problems his problems, and he has also made his resources our resources.

Another example of one person's responsibility being transferred to someone else is adoption. At the moment of adoption, adoptive parents become responsible for what their child does. If he breaks a neighbor's window, the parents are held responsible. If he steals, the parents pay. By the act of adoption, the parents take on the responsibility for that child as long as he is under their care. Even when the child is the guilty one and the parents have no part in wrongdoing, they are liable. They pay the price.

That may give us a hint of how Jesus could be held liable for sins he didn't commit, for sins we've committed. The Bible tells us that in Christ, God has adopted us as his sons and daughters. This adoption is possible only because God, in the person of Jesus, has taken upon himself the responsibility for our sins.

It Is Finished

God's holy wrath against sin requires that when somebody sins, somebody pays. Every sinner must either be punished or else have his sin atoned for by the sacrificial death of another. The responsibility for our guilt was transferred to Jesus, and he paid the penalty we owed when he suffered the agony of hell on the cross. Only such a sacrifice could bring people back to God.

In the eyes of God, the cross was really an altar. The blood streaming from Jesus' wounds wasn't just the draining of his physical life but also the offering of a spiritual payment to atone for the sins of the world (1 John 2:2). After that sacrifice, God never again required animal sacrifice; and, as always, he rejected any human sacrifice except the sacrifice of his own Son. Jesus' death is of infinite value. It's more than enough to pay for all your sins and mine and everyone else's. Jesus paid the price of sin once for all. No other sacrifice for sin will ever be needed.

Just before Jesus died, he cried out, "It is finished" (John 19:30). That wasn't just an expression of relief that death would bring his suffering to an end. When Jesus said, "It is finished," he meant that he had finished doing everything necessary to make people right with God. He had lived a perfect life, had suffered in place of others, and had given his blood to pay for their sins. In Jesus' time, the declaration "it is finished" was commonly used in the business world to mean "paid in full." Through Jesus' suffering, the penalty for sin was paid in full. Nothing more needed to be done. Nothing more was owed. Nobody else needed to suffer.

"God presented him as a sacrifice of atonement, through faith in his blood" (Romans 3:25). Believe this good news. Believe that God accepts you in love for Jesus' sake. Believe that Jesus' blood pays for your sin and cancels your guilt. Let Jesus satisfy your deep inner craving for atonement. By faith in Christ's atonement, be free from the dreadful drive to punish yourself. Be free from the urge to blame and punish others to make yourself feel better. Be free to rejoice in God's love for you, and be free to love others.

Chapter 12

Going to the Doctor

Some people avoid doctors. No matter how sick they get, they'd rather tough it out than go to the doctor. Maybe you're like that. You could have one foot in the grave and the other on a banana peel, and you'd still avoid going to the doctor.

Why are some of us are so reluctant to go to the doctor? For some it might be a matter of money. If you don't have full insurance, a visit to the doctor might cost you, and you'd rather wait and see whether you get better on your own.

For others, staying away from the doctor is a matter of pride. You're not a wimp. You don't panic over every hangnail or runny nose. You don't rush off to the emergency room for every little thing, like some people you know.

Then again, you might have a completely different reason for not going to the doctor: fear. If you notice a strange blotch on your skin, or feel pain in your stomach day after day, or find a suspicious lump, you're scared. You try to convince yourself that maybe it's nothing. You figure that if you just wait a few more days, maybe it will go away. You can't bear the thought of going to the doctor and hearing the word *cancer*. Of course, the sooner you see the doctor, the more likely it is that the disease will still be treatable—you know that, but you wait anyway. It's not rational to wait, but who ever said fear is rational?

Still, when something is really wrong with you, you need to see a doctor. No matter how much you drag your feet, no matter what reasons you have for staying away, there are times when a doctor is the only person who can diagnose what's wrong and provide a cure. So if you haven't been feeling quite right and you've been putting off going for help—please, quit stalling and go to the doctor.

But even if you don't need a doctor just now, I want you to think with me about going to the doctor in another sense. Jesus is sometimes called "the Great Physician." When Jesus walked this earth, he healed all sorts of diseases and disabilities. He made the lame to walk, the deaf to hear, the blind to see. But his greatest miracle of healing—a miracle he still does today—is that he takes sinful people whose prognosis is certain death, and he conquers their sin, cures them of the evil that is destroying them, and gives them eternal life.

Unfortunately, as reluctant as many of us are to go to a medical doctor, we're even more reluctant to go to the divine Doctor. We may stay away from Jesus for much the same reasons we avoid ordinary doctors. We may worry that it will cost us something; we don't want to go to Jesus if he might require us to give up something for his sake. Or we may stay away because of pride; we want to prove we can make it on our own without admitting we need Christ's help. Or we may avoid Christ because of fear; we're afraid he'll tell us we're in bad shape. We don't want to deal with guilt and fear of judgment, and we're not confident he'll help us. But whatever holds us back from going to Jesus, we need to go to him anyway.

When we go to Jesus as the Great Physician, what should we expect? Well, what do you expect when you go to an ordinary doctor? First, you want an accurate diagnosis. If something is ailing you, you want to know what it is. And once the problem is diagnosed, you obviously want something else: you want a cure. You want the doctor to do whatever it takes to make you healthy again. Diagnosis and cure—these two things are what you expect and hope for when you go to the doctor, and that's what to look for when you go to Jesus.

The Diagnosis

Let's focus first on diagnosis. When Jesus explained why he came into the world, he pictured himself as a doctor and people as his patients. Jesus said, "It is not the healthy who need a doctor, but the sick. I have not come to call the righteous, but sinners" (Mark 2:17). Here is the Lord's diagnosis of our situation: we are sick and sinful. Unless something changes, we are doomed to eternal death in hell. You can't get a more devastating diagnosis than that.

You might ask, "How do we know? Does God have any way of showing us?" Yes, he does—his law. God's moral law shows us how unhealthy we are. We may get some sense of our condition through the inner law of our conscience (Romans 2:14-15), but the clearest, most reliable test is God's written law found in the Bible, especially in the Ten Commandments.

Think for a moment of bodily sickness. How can you tell when you have a bad illness? One way is how you feel. If you feel fine, you usually assume you're healthy, but if you feel pain, you figure something is wrong. That's sort of how conscience works. When you feel stabs of guilt and shame, your painful conscience may be telling you something is wrong.

But what if your conscience doesn't bother you? Does that mean you're okay? Not necessarily. Conscience isn't 100 percent reliable. You may do something without a twinge of conscience, without the least bit of moral uneasiness, and still be wrong.

Think again of how your body works. Sometimes, when something is wrong, you feel pain. But it's possible to feel no pain at all and yet have a deadly condition. A routine checkup at the doctor may reveal cancer or heart trouble or a virus like HIV, even if you don't feel anything wrong. In the latter stages of the illness, pain may kick in, but meanwhile, the fact that you're *feeling* healthy is no guarantee that you *are* healthy. Sometimes sin can be painless for a while. In some cases, stabs of conscience may tell you something's wrong with you, or huge problems like a prison sentence or a divorce or a sexually transmitted disease may show you something is wrong. But even if your conscience doesn't bother you, even if you're not facing a crisis because of bad behavior, you may still have a deadly problem. Pain can be a warning sign, but it's not as reliable as a more objective test.

The objective test of your spiritual health is the written law of God found in the Bible. Just as an objective medical test can diagnose a deadly illness you didn't know you had, so the objective standards of God's law can show you sins you didn't know you had. As a biblical writer puts it, "I would not have known what sin was except through the law" (Romans 7:7).

God's law commands, "You shall have no other gods before me," so if you put anything ahead of God, it means you're sick. The law says not to misuse God's name, so if you ever curse or swear, you're sick. The law says not to murder or hate, so if you ever hate or resent, you're sick. The law says not to commit adultery (and Jesus explains that this means you must not even lust). If you do, you're sick. The law condemns stealing, so whenever you copy software or videos you haven't paid for, it means you're sick. The law prohibits lying, so every time you deceive someone else, it means you're sick. God's law commands us to love God above all and to love our neighbor as ourselves—and as Jesus explains it, our neighbor includes even our enemy. Anything less than that kind of love means you're sick. The objective test of God's law shows that all of us are sick with sin. And sin, left to run its course, results in death (Romans 6:21,23), not just physical death but what the Bible calls "the second death," eternal suffering in hell.

You may be tempted to say, "No way! It can't be that bad. I'm basically a good person, and my conscience feels fine. Sure, nobody's perfect, but I'm better than most people. I know what really rotten sinners are like, and I'm not one of them."

It's understandable if you feel that way, but think about it. Suppose you're tested and confirmed to have cancer. You might protest, "No way! I feel fine. Just look at me. I'm the picture of health. Besides, I know what cancer does to people. I've seen cancer victims. I've seen how sick they get and how miserable they feel, and I'm not that way at all. I can't have cancer." All of that doesn't change the result of the objective test. If you have cancer, you have cancer. Focusing on how well you feel won't help. Comparisons to others won't help. There's no such thing as "a mild case" of cancer. If you have it and nothing is done about it, it will kill you.

Sin is like cancer. You may think your sins are small, but if God's law turns up even the slightest trace of sin in your life, you have a huge problem. "For whoever keeps the whole law and yet stumbles at just one point is guilty of breaking all of it" (James 2:10). If God's law diagnoses you as a sinner in any respect, the size of the sin or the number of sins is almost beside the point. If you've got sin anywhere in your system, you're doomed if nothing is done about it, just as a person who's got cancer anywhere in his system is doomed if nothing is done about it.

Some years ago my father went to the doctor. He felt fine, but it was time for his annual checkup. A routine test found cancer in an early stage. The doctor recommended surgery. Would it be foolish for someone who feels perfectly well to go through the pain and bother of surgery? Well, my dad had the surgery. He believed his doctor and accepted the test results, even though he felt fine. Since then he has been cancer-free.

If a doctor says you're sick and the test shows it, then regardless of how you feel, you'd better believe it and have him do something about it. Likewise, if the Lord says you're sinful and his law shows it, then regardless of how you feel, you'd better believe it and have him do something about it.

The Cure

The Great Physician not only gives you the diagnosis, he also provides the cure. What is the cure for sin? You may be tempted to think God's law is the cure—if only you can do better in living up to it. But no, God's law can't cure sin. The law is great for diagnosing the problem but not for curing it.

A medical test is useful for showing whether you have cancer, but the test can't cure you. It only diagnoses your illness. It's good that there's a test, but if that's all there is, the cancer will kill you. So too, it's good that we have God's law to diagnose our sin, but if that's all we have, we will perish. We need something besides the law to save us.

The great news of the Bible, the marvelous message of the gospel, is that God himself has provided exactly the cure we need. "For what the law was powerless to do, God did by sending his own Son" (Romans 8:2). Our cure is found in the person of Jesus.

Jesus went around calling even the worst of sinners to follow him, enter God's kingdom, and be his friends. He had meals with lowlifes of every kind. He welcomed one and all to find in him God's forgiveness and eternal life.

Some of the more religious and respectable people were shocked by Jesus' behavior. They thought they could save themselves by keeping God's law. They fooled themselves into thinking that because their sins weren't quite as obvious as some people's, they were okay. They thought that when they did have a sin or two, their rituals would make up for it. They felt no need for Jesus, and they were scandalized that such a famous teacher would associate with such despicable people.

When the Pharisees complained and asked why Jesus would associate with such awful sinners, Jesus said to them, "It is not the healthy who need a doctor, but the sick. I have not come to call the righteous, but sinners" (Mark 2:17). Jesus didn't come to earth to set up a tennis club for splendid spiritual specimens. He came to bring healing to sick people who desperately need a doctor. He came because we're all sinners in need of a Savior.

Ultimately Jesus went all the way to the cross and death in order to cure us. He poured out his blood and gave up his life to overcome our sin and give us new life. "By his wounds we are healed" (Isaiah 53:5). At this point, of course, what Jesus did to save us goes far beyond what we can picture by comparing him to a doctor. We might want a doctor to be gentle and have a nice bedside manner, but we don't expect a doctor to love us enough to die for us. When doctors help sick people, they often get paid a lot for doing so, but Jesus didn't get paid. He himself paid the cost of his own life in order to provide a cure for us.

The closest medical comparison might be an organ donor. I know someone with a family member whose kidneys were failing. She wanted to save her loved one, so she donated one of her own kidneys, at great pain and risk to herself, so that it could be transplanted into the one she loved. Jesus went beyond even that. He gave his entire body and his very life in order to save us. Like people with heart trouble who can receive a heart transplant only if another person dies, you and I can receive the spiritual heart transplant we need only because Someone else died—our Lord Jesus Christ. Somehow, in the miracle of God's grace, when you trust in Jesus, his blood takes away your sin, his death rescues you from hell, his wounds heal your soul, his Spirit gives you a new heart, and his resurrection gives you eternal life.

And that's not all. Jesus not only overcomes your illness and gives you new life, but he also gives you a whole new immune system. Think of what happens if your body's immune system doesn't work. Just about any infection or illness can kill you. But with a healthy immune system, you catch far fewer infections, and even if you catch one from time to time, you can overcome it. Your body has the power to fight back. Apart from Jesus, you have no spiritual immune system; any sin at all is fatal. But when you come to Jesus, he not only cancels the penalty of your sin, but he also gives you the power of his Holy Spirit.

The Holy Spirit fights against sin the way your immune system fights against infections. When you sin, it upsets your system, but it can no longer kill you, because you have within you the power of the Holy Spirit to attack that sin and overcome it. As long as you're in this world, you'll have sins to deal with. You won't be perfect until you get to heaven. But when you belong to Jesus, his Spirit guarantees that you will live forever, he gives you the power to survive your bouts with sin, and he empowers you to grow stronger and healthier the longer he lives in you.

Your Response

The blood of Jesus and renewal by the Holy Spirit are God's cure for sin—the only cure. So how about it? Have you gone to the doctor? Have you submitted to his diagnosis and admitted that you're a sinner? Have you accepted God's cure and put your trust in Jesus? Have you prayed for pardon through Jesus' blood and received his Holy Spirit? If you want to be cured of sin and live forever, that's the only way.

Maybe that offends you. You may think there should be many ways to be saved. You may think it's unfair of God to offer only one. But think about it. Suppose someone discovered a cure for every form of cancer. Suppose it was a pill with a taste some people didn't like but which cured anyone who swallowed it and was offered for free to anyone who wanted it. Do you think people would complain and say, "That's not fair. There should be a lot of cures, not just one with a taste I don't like." No way! If someone discovered a cure for cancer, cancer patients would all shout for joy and rush to the nearest place the cure was available. Nobody would complain that this was the only cure. One cure is a lot better than none!

So why complain when faith in Jesus' blood is the only cure for sin? One cure is a lot better than none. None is what Christ owed us; one is what he gave us. So don't complain or look for other cures. Instead, accept the amazing cure that God freely gives us at such great cost to himself.

Maybe you have a different reason for not going to Jesus and becoming part of his church. You know people who call themselves Christians, and some of them are pretty bad. You know church members who are a long way from perfect. Now, I don't want to make any excuse for sin, and I know how hurtful these things can be, but let me just ask: What do you expect? If you go to the hospital, do you expect everybody there to be perfectly healthy? It's a hospital, not a tennis club! So if you're a sinner in need of healing, don't be shocked if you go to church and find other sinners. The church of Jesus is a group of people who are looking to the Great Physician for their healing. Are you too good for them? Do you want to be a Pharisee who stays away because Jesus has too many sinners around him? "It is not the healthy who need a doctor, but the sick."

Maybe you're saying, "I'd like Jesus to save me, but I don't know if I can make my faith strong enough. I have so many doubts and misgivings." But you don't need a strong faith in order to be saved. You just need a strong Savior. If you're sick and you go to a good doctor, it doesn't much matter if you feel hesitation and uncertainty. What matters is simply that you go, and that he's a doctor who can really help you. If you decided to go to Dr. Quack and took his magic wonder potion, you could feel all the confidence in the world, but it wouldn't help you get over a serious illness. What matters most is going to the right doctor, not having the right feelings. You're better off with a weak faith in a strong Savior than with a strong faith in anything else. Don't worry if your faith is weak and sick. You're just the sort of person Jesus wants to help. "It is not the healthy who need a doctor but the sick." Your faith may be sick and shaking with doubt, but as long as Jesus is the one you go to, he will save you.

Chapter 13

Trinity of Love

"In the beginning God created the heavens and the earth" (Genesis 1:1). That's the first sentence of the Bible. But who created God? The answer is that nobody created God. The Lord has always existed. He had no beginning and will have no end.

But that raises more questions. What did God do before he started creating? Was God all alone before creation, with nothing to do and nobody to relate to? Wouldn't that get to be boring and lonely? Children wonder about questions like that, and so do some grownups.

A child who asks what God did before he made the world is onto something important. The child senses that there's a problem with thinking of God as a single, solitary individual who just happens to be stronger, smarter, purer and much older than everyone else. If we picture God simply as the great, divine individual who made everything, then we can't help thinking that if he weren't dealing with creation, he'd be doing nothing; and that if he didn't have any creatures, he'd be all alone.

Then we might take the next step and conclude that God made the world to escape boredom and to give himself something to do, and that he made other individuals so that he'd have someone to relate to. What else would there be for God to do if he weren't dealing with his creation? And how could a single, solitary God love and be loved apart from created beings?

The true answer to all this is that God does not exist as a single, solitary individual. God is a union of three divine Persons: the Father, the Son, and the Holy Spirit. These three divine Persons are eternally united in love and in the very essence of their being. Father, Son, and Spirit eternally have one another to love and to enjoy. Each one has such an infinity of wisdom, beauty, goodness, and vitality that it would be impossible for Father, Son, and Spirit to feel bored with one another. Each gives and receives such an infinity of love that it would be impossible for Father, Son, and Spirit to feel lonely or in need of love.

What was God doing before he made the world? If I may say so reverently, God was busy being God and enjoying it immensely. From eternity Father, Son, and Spirit share a richness of being so full that no other being can add to it. From eternity Father, Son, and Spirit share such a mutual love that no other love is needed.

God Is Love

That puts the creation and all of God's dealings with his creatures in a new light. God created all things and relates to his creatures not to address some lack in his being but to express a great overflow of his being. God formed this vast and varied creation not because he would otherwise be bored but because he is bountiful. God takes a personal interest in his creatures not because he would otherwise be lonely but because he is love. "God is love" (1 John 4:16). Those are perhaps the most beautiful words in the Bible. But to sense the full impact and to be in touch with the reality those words describe, we need to know how Father, Son, and Holy Spirit relate to one another in the being of God, and how Father, Son, and Spirit relate to us.

The Bible doesn't just say that God loves, but that God *is* love. Love is who God is, even apart from the creatures he has made. God is love, and that can't be true unless the being of God involves more than one Person. "Love is something that one person has for another person. If God was a single person, then before the world was made, He was not love" (C.S. Lewis). But God is love, and so God is more than one Person. God is love because God is Trinity: Father, Son, and Holy Spirit, three Persons united in mutual, eternal love.

It was out of a surplus of love—not a shortage of love—that this great God said, "Let us make man in our image, in our likeness" (Genesis 1:26). God created us for love: to be loved by him, to love him in return, and to love one another.

However, with our fall into sin, we messed things up. We cut ourselves off from God. We broke the rhythm of love and became self-centered. So what has God done? Has he simply cast humanity away? No, he loves the world so much that he's gone to the trouble of rescuing us. Father, Son, and Spirit each play a distinctive part in this great rescue and at the same time are fully united in accomplishing our salvation.

The final goal of creation and salvation is this: that we be caught up into the love and life of God—Father, Son, and Holy Spirit—and become "partakers of the divine nature" (2 Peter 1:4). It's a staggering thought, but it's true. Believing in the blessed Trinity of love and being drawn up into the eternal life of Father, Son, and Spirit—this is the very heart of Christianity.

Difficult Doctrine

You may be thinking to yourself, "That sounds complicated. Why bother with a confusing idea like three in one? Why bother with doctrine at all? Don't get me wrong: I'm a spiritual person. I believe in God. I've even felt him. But I don't need dry, difficult doctrine. Experience is better than doctrine."

Well, there's a measure of truth in that. I'd rather be in touch with God than merely bat around certain ideas about him. But look at it this way. Suppose there's a really great person you want to get to know better, and so far you've only had the opportunity to shake hands with him. Should you focus only on how you felt in that electrifying moment when you shook hands? Shouldn't you also listen to what people say who know the person better than you do? And even more important, shouldn't you listen to what the person says about himself, and take note of the things that he does? That may do more to help you really know him and develop a relationship with him than simply feeling aglow about the fact that you once shook his hand.

Or look at it from another angle. C. S. Lewis observes that if a person has an experience of God's majesty in nature, the experience may very well be real; and if the person then turns from experience to Christian doctrines, he is in a sense turning from something real to something less real.

In the same way, if a man has once looked at the Atlantic from the beach, and then goes and looks at a map of the Atlantic, he also will be turning from something real to something less real: turning from real waves to a bit of coloured paper. But here comes the point. The map is admittedly only coloured paper, but there are two things you have to remember about it. In the first place, it is based on what hundreds and thousands of people have found out by sailing the real Atlantic. In that way it has behind it masses of experiences just as real as the one you could have from the beach; only, while yours would be a single isolated glimpse, the map fits all those different experiences together. In the second place, if you want to go anywhere, the map is absolutely necessary. As long as you are content with walks on the beach your own glimpses are far more fun than looking at a map. But the map is going to be more use than walks on the beach if you want to [cross the ocean to another land].

Doctrines aren't God. They're just a map. But let's remember two things about that doctrinal map. First, it's based on the experience of many people who were in touch with God. In fact, their mighty encounters with Father, Son, and Holy Spirit would make any experience of yours or mine seem small and confused. Second, remember that if you want to get any further in your relationship with God, you need the map.

A certain experience you've had may be real and even exciting, "but nothing comes of it. It leads nowhere. There is nothing to do about it. In fact, that is just why a vague religion—all about God in nature and so on—is so attractive. It is all thrills and no work; like watching the waves from the beach" (C. S. Lewis). But you will not set sail or reach another land by watching the waves, and you will not get eternal life by simply feeling the presence of God in flowers or music. You need the doctrines, the truth about God, to map out the way, and you need to be caught up into the life of God. Of course, if you only talk about God and never meet him, you won't have fellowship with God and eternal life—doctrine without personal involvement leads nowhere. But neither will you have true fellowship with God if all you do is cling to a feeling you once got when you met him briefly. You must get to know him better. You must learn who he is, what he's like, what he's done, and what he wants to make of you.

Listen to the words of Jesus himself. After he rose from the dead and before he ascended to heaven, Jesus told his followers, "Go and make disciples of all nations, baptizing them in the name of the Father and of the Son and of the Holy Spirit, and teaching them to obey everything I have commanded you" (Matthew 28:19). Jesus doesn't just want people to "have experiences." He wants people to belong to him, to be his disciples, to obey him. Also, Jesus doesn't want people to muddle along with an indefinite sense of the God they belong to. He wants them to be baptized and marked with a definite name—the name of the Father and of the Son and of the Holy Spirit. Jesus doesn't say "in the *names*" of Father, Son, and Spirit, but "in the *name*." The threefold title *Father, Son, and Holy Spirit*—is the name of the one true God.

What God Reveals

Every major branch of the Christian church teaches the doctrine of the Trinity. According to this doctrine, God forever exists as three divine Persons: Father, Son, and Holy Spirit. Each Person is fully God. Yet there is only one God. As the Athanasian Creed puts it: "The Father is God, the Son is God, the Holy Spirit is God. Yet there are not three gods; there is but one God." Is that good theology, or just bad math? Already when you're small, you learn that one plus one plus one equals three. But it sounds like, in order to be a Christian and believe in the

Trinity, you have to believe that one plus one plus one equals one. That doesn't seem to make much sense. Why would anyone who believes in three divine Persons keep insisting that there is only one God? Why would anyone who understands simple arithmetic believe in the Trinity?

The reason Christians believe in the Trinity is that this is how God has revealed himself. The doctrine of the Trinity isn't something that anybody could have dreamed up. It is a response to God's self-revelation. It's the church's best effort to map out what God reveals about himself. God reveals his nature as Trinity in the coming of God's Son in human flesh and in the outpouring of the Holy Spirit into human hearts. God's nature as Trinity is displayed in these actions of God, it's written in the Bible, it's professed in the church, and it's experienced in the lives of Christians.

Anybody who believes in one God would have no problem granting that the invisible, eternal Father is God. But some might question the deity of Jesus or the Holy Spirit. They might say that Jesus is less than God and that the Holy Spirit is only God's power, not a divine Person, and that the Father is therefore the only one who can truly be called God. But the Bible plainly teaches that both Jesus and the Holy Spirit are divine and personal, along with God the Father.

Referring to Jesus as "the Word," John 1:1 says, "The Word was God." Jesus acted as God's equal when he exercised authority to forgive sins and when he commanded the forces of nature through various miracles. In talking to his Father in heaven, Jesus said, "Father, glorify me in your presence with the glory I had before the world began" (John 17:5). Jesus told some religious leaders, "Before Abraham was, I AM!" (John 8:58). He existed from all eternity as God the Son, before Abraham was ever born. Indeed, the reason the religious leaders gave for crucifying Jesus was that he claimed to be equal with God. And Jesus proved himself to be the Son of God in power when he rose from the dead. After Jesus' resurrection, Thomas said to him, "My Lord and my God!" (John 20:28).

The Bible also shows that the Holy Spirit is God. The Bible's formulas for baptism and blessing include the Holy Spirit along with the Father and the Son. How could that be so, unless the Holy Spirit is also God? The Bible often refers to the Holy Spirit as "the Spirit of God." Some who deny the Trinity argue that the Spirit is not a Person but is just a force, the impersonal power of God. But Jesus spoke of the Holy Spirit as a Person, a Comforter or Advocate (John 14:16,26; 15:2; 16:7). Peter said that lying to the Holy Spirit was lying to God (Acts 5:3-4). Elsewhere the Bible warns, "Do not grieve the Holy Spirit of God" (Ephesians 4:30). You can't lie to a force; you can only lie to a person. You can't grieve a power; you can only grieve a person. The Holy Spirit is not just a force. He is a Person, and he is God.

The Bible shows that three distinct Persons are God, yet the Bible also reveals that God is one. The oneness of God is taught clearly throughout the Bible, beginning in the Old Testament. Deuteronomy 6:4 says, "Hear, O Israel, the Lord our God, the Lord is one." In Isaiah 46:9 the Lord says, "I am God, and there is no other." The New Testament also insists that there is only one God. 1 Corinthians 8:4 declares, "We know that an idol is nothing at all in the world and that there is no God but one."

There you have it: the Father is God, the Son is God, and the Holy Spirit is God. There are three divine Persons, yet these three are somehow united as one God. When Christians speak of the Trinity, it's not that we don't understand arithmetic. It's that the God who has existed from everlasting to everlasting is much greater than any notions about him that we might come up with on our own, and he has revealed himself to be one God in three Persons. The inspired writings of the Bible explain and confirm what the actions of God in history have shown: the reality of one God in three Persons.

In response to God's actions and his Word, the church professes and celebrates the triune God. Every time someone becomes part of the church through baptism, that person is baptized "in the name of the Father, and of the Son, and of the Holy Spirit," as Jesus commanded. When Christians receive God's

blessing in the church, the person leading the worship pro-
nounces the blessing in the name of the Father, the Son, and the
Holy Spirit. Often it's a direct quote from a blessing in the Bible,
which says, "May the grace of the Lord Jesus Christ, and the love
of God, and the fellowship of the Holy Spirit be with you all" (2
Corinthians 13:14). The Christian church declares, in the words
of the Athanasian Creed: "The Father is God, the Son is God,
the Holy Spirit is God. Yet there are not three gods; there is but
one God."

Trying to Understand

Christians believe one God in three Persons. Christians believe that God is three in a certain sense, but in another sense he
is one. But what does this mean? And why does it matter?

One of the easiest solutions is to say that there is really only
one Person who is God, and that "Father," "Son," and "Holy
Spirit" are just three different titles for three different modes in
which the one God operates.

For example, I am one person with several different roles and
titles. I'm "Dave" to my friends, "Dad" to my children, and
"Pastor" to many other people. It's easy to see that although
"Dave" is David Feddes, "Dad" is David Feddes, and "Pastor" is
also David Feddes, there are not three persons, but one. Those
three titles simply refer to one man, myself, who has the three
roles of friend, father, and minister.

Is that what the Trinity is? Are Father, Son, and Holy Spirit
simply three roles played by the same divine Person, who is
called Father in his work of creating and caring for people; called
the Son, or Jesus, when he is providing forgiveness of sin and
victory over death; and called the Holy Spirit in his work of living within Christians and making them more holy? No, the
Trinity is not just one Person with three different roles. God has
far more than three roles and titles, but God is exactly three Persons: Father, Son, and Holy Spirit.

Another variation on seeing God as one Person in three different modes deals with different phases in God's career, so to

speak. In this approach, talking about God the Father, God the Son, and God the Holy Spirit would be similar to talking about Barack Obama the professor, Barack Obama the Senator, and Barack Obama the President. There have not been three Barack Obamas but just one, whose life includes these three different career phases.

Some people have mistakenly thought of the Trinity in a similar way, viewing God as one divine Person who has existed in three major phases. Originally, he was the almighty, invisible Father. Then, about 2,000 years ago, he moved out of that phase to become a human being, Jesus, until his resurrection and ascension. Then, on Pentecost, God entered a new phase when he came upon the church as the Holy Spirit. But is this all that the Bible means when it teaches that Father, Son, and Holy Spirit are one God? No, Father, Son, and Holy Spirit are three divine *Persons*, not just one Person in different phases.

Father, Son, and Holy Spirit—that's who God is and always was and always will be. God was Trinity before the creation of the world. All three Persons have existed together from all eternity. The Son of God entered Mary's womb and was born in a stable, but that is not when he began to exist or when he became the Son of the Father for the first time. That's when God took on a human nature, but before coming into the world as a baby, God the Son existed with God the Father from all eternity. Likewise, the Spirit of God did not begin to exist on the day of Pentecost. That is when he came upon Jesus' followers with great power and filled them with the life of God, but the Holy Spirit has forever proceeded from the union of Father and Son. The Spirit is from eternity the third Person in the being of God.

Father, Son, and Holy Spirit are not all the same Person. After Jesus was baptized, "he saw the Spirit of God descending like a dove and lighting on him. And a voice from heaven said, 'This is my Son, whom I love; with him I am well pleased.'" (Matthew 3:16-17). The voice from heaven was God the Father speaking to his Son; it wasn't Jesus acting as a ventriloquist and causing a voice from heaven to talk about himself. Also, the Spirit who descended on Jesus is not the same Person as Jesus. The Bible clearly teaches that Father, Son, and Holy Spirit are distinct Persons, and that each of these Persons is fully divine.

One God, Not Many

If Christians believe that Father, Son, and Holy Spirit—three distinct Persons—are God, why don't we just state the obvious and say there are three Gods? When the Greeks said that Zeus, Apollo, and Hermes were all gods, they didn't pretend that these three were somehow one God. So how are Father, Son, and Spirit one God, any more than the gods of ancient myth?

For starters, the Bible teaches equality of the three Persons within the oneness of God. In the legends, one god was the chief deity in the pecking order. For the Greeks, it was Zeus who had the most power; for the Romans, it was Jupiter; for the Vikings, it was Odin. In contrast to all this, no Person in the Trinity lacks any divine attributes of the others or is inferior. Father, Son, and Holy Spirit are all equally infinite in power, splendor, wisdom, love, and holiness. All are equally eternal, uncreated, without beginning or end. This is true because all three Persons share the same divine essence.

Another obvious difference between the one triune God and the false gods is that in the Trinity there is a complete oneness of will, a total unity of purpose, a perfect harmony. Father, Son, and Spirit never disagree or squabble. That's a far cry from the mythical gods who were constantly bickering and doing things behind each other's backs. In the oneness of will that exists in the Trinity, the Son never contradicts the Father's will. Never does the Father want one thing, the Son want another, and the Spirit something else. Jesus the Son came to do the will of his Father. Likewise, the Holy Spirit always does his work in perfect cooperation with the purposes of the Father and the Son. Father, Son, and Holy Spirit are one in will and purpose.

The oneness of God also means that there is no division of authority, where each divine Person controls a different aspect of life. In the ancient superstitions, one god would be the god of war, another the god of sex and fertility, another the god of wisdom, and so forth. So, depending on what you needed at the time, you would try to get on the good side of the particular god who controlled that part of life. The great truth that God is one means that he is Lord over every part of life, not just some specialty. He is Creator and Master of all things.

Since God is one, you can't get out of his territory and into the territory of a god who will perhaps be different. Father, Son, and Holy Spirit don't each rule different parts of the universe. The Trinity rules as one God with no division of territory. The Bible tells about a time when the Lord helped his people to win a battle over superior forces. The people opposing them weren't about to give up, however. They figured that they had lost the first battle only because it had been fought in the hills. The enemy king's officials advised him, "Their gods are gods of the hills. That is why they were too strong for us. But if we fight them on the plains, surely we will be stronger than they" (1 Kings 20:23). They figured a god who controlled what happened in the hills might not be so strong on the plains, so they fought the next battle on the plains—and suffered an even worse defeat than before. They learned the hard way that there is just one God who is equally in charge on both hills and plains.

God's Word simply won't permit us to talk about three gods, even though there are three divine Persons. Father, Son, and Holy Spirit are united in full and equal deity; they are united in will and purpose; they are united in joint reign over all things. And the oneness of the Trinity transcends even these aspects of unity. There is a unity within the Trinity which underlies these things, and which is deeper, stronger, and also more mysterious.

The Bible compels us to believe that the three divine Persons share in the same divine being or essence. Father, Son, and Holy Spirit are not the same Person, but they are united in the same being. They are distinct from one another, but never divided or separated or independent from each other. All three share the same divine essence and are united as one divine being, from eternity past, right now, and into the eternal future.

More Than Personal

We're used to thinking of persons as separate individuals, so we can hardly imagine how three persons could be one being. But why should we suppose that God can be reduced to our level and understood in our terms? Not only is God personal, he's more than personal. God is not just one Person but a superpersonal union of three divine Persons. C.S. Lewis writes,

> The human level is a simple and rather empty level. On the human level one person is one being, and any two persons are two separate beings... On the Divine level you still find personalities; but up there you find them combined in ways which we, who do not live on that level, cannot imagine.
>
> A good many people nowadays say, 'I believe in a God, but not in a personal God.' They feel that the mysterious something which is behind all other things must be more than a person. And in a sense they are right about this. But although they say God is beyond personality, they end up thinking of him as something impersonal, as a vague sort of power, or as a great void: that is, as something less than personal.

Christians are the only people with any idea of a being beyond personality: more than personal, not less than personal. Christians know that God is more than a person; God is a superpersonal union of three divine Persons. And therefore God is not just a power; God is love. It is out of the overflow of God's love that he created the world. It is out of the overflow of God's love that he redeemed his people by sending his Son to live a perfect human life, die a terrible death, and rise again for their salvation. It is out of the overflow of God's love that his Holy Spirit comes into the hearts of believers and floods them with the love and life of the Holy Trinity.

The deep and mysterious oneness of God's being is related to a marvelous oneness of love, a love that has forever united the Persons of the Trinity with each other. There is no way we can fully describe or understand this union of Father, Son, and Spirit, since God transcends any earthly comparison we might use. But maybe we can get a hint of this unifying love if we think of a husband and wife who have enjoyed a long, loving marriage. Sometimes both have the same thought at the same time, or one knows how the other is feeling without being told. They've been together so long, loving each other so much, knowing each other so well, that sometimes they almost think, feel, and act as one.

Now take that and multiply it infinitely. The love among Father, Son, and Holy Spirit is immeasurably greater than the love of a husband and wife. Not only that, but Father, Son, and Holy Spirit have existed together in perfect harmony, not just for several decades, but for all eternity. When the Bible says "God is love," it's not just because God is loving toward us but also because God's inner being is characterized by the eternal love that unites Father, Son, and Holy Spirit. The three divine Persons are forever united by their mutual love and also in the very substance of their being.

Relating to God

Even after we know something of the reality of the Trinity, we still confront a great mystery. The being of God is a blazing light that we can't look at directly or figure out completely. We'll go blind if we try. But, like the sun, this blazing light of God enlightens and warms everything it touches. The Trinity is hard to explain; the Trinity is hard even to imagine; and yet the Trinity is the one true God, the only God worth worshiping.

It is impossible to have a right relationship with God while being part of a religion which denies the Trinity and doesn't accept Christ as divine. I've heard it said, "Even if some people don't believe in Jesus, at least we all believe in the same God." Is that so? How can you reject Jesus and be right with God the Father? If you don't love Jesus, you can't love the Father. Jesus declared, "He who hates me hates my Father as well" (John 15:23). We don't all believe in the same God. Any religion that rejects the Trinity rejects God, because the Trinity is God. There is no God apart from the union of Father, Son, and Spirit.

In order to have a healthy relationship with God, we must know who God is and how to come to him. Jesus says, "No one comes to the Father except through me" (John 14:6), and he also says, "No one can come to me unless the Father who sent me draws him" (John 6:44). Salvation is a work involving the Father and the Son. And the Father and Son do nothing apart from the Holy Spirit. "If anyone does not have the Spirit of Christ, he does not belong to Christ" (Romans 8:9).

Each Person of the Trinity is essential in the work of salvation and in establishing God's kingdom of love. Ultimately, God's purpose is that his people become one in love in a way that somehow reflects the loving oneness of the Trinity (John 17:11). God is love, both in the eternal love that the Persons of the Trinity have for each other, and in the way God relates to his people. There is nothing more wonderful or more necessary than to be drawn into living faith in this marvelous God.

Even though you can't understand the deeper mysteries of the Trinity, you experience the life of the Trinity whenever you pray as a Christian. In prayer the one you're trying to get in touch with is God. And what is prompting you to pray is also God: the Spirit inside you. And you come to God through Christ, who connects God and humanity. See what's happening? God is the one to whom you're praying, the goal you're trying to reach. God is also the one inside you who is pushing you along. God is also the road or the bridge along which you're being pushed toward that goal. Praying to the Father, prompted by the Holy Spirit, through the Son, Jesus Christ—this is fellowship with the Trinity of love. In our minds we can't fully understand, but in our hearts we can bow down in worship before the majesty and mystery of these three infinite, magnificent, eternal Persons united in a perfect oneness that surpasses all human imagination or description. And we can look forward to the day when we will no longer see dimly but see clearly and directly, and have all of eternity to enjoy the life and love of the blessed Trinity.

Chapter 14

Why Does God Hide?

If God exists, and if he wants everybody to believe in him, why does he hide? Why doesn't he show himself or do something so spectacular that it leaves no room for doubt?

Many of us wonder about that. The late philosopher N. R. Hanson didn't believe in God, but he said he'd be willing to change his mind under certain conditions. Hanson wrote:

Suppose that on next Tuesday morning, just after breakfast, all of us in this one world are knocked to our knees by a percussive and ear-shattering thunderclap. Snow swirls; leaves drop from trees; the earth heaves and buckles; buildings topple and towers tumble; the sky is ablaze with an eerie, silvery light. Just then, as all the people of this world look up, the heavens open—the clouds pull apart—revealing an unbelievably immense and radiant Zeus-like figure, towering above us like a hundred Everests. He frowns darkly as lightning plays across the features of his Michelangeloid face. He then points down— *at me*—and exclaims for every man, woman, and child to hear, "I have had quite enough of your too-clever logic-chopping and word-watching in matters of theology. Be assured, N. R. Hanson, that I do most certainly exist."

Hanson went on to say, "Please do not dismiss this example as a playful, irreverent Disney-oid contrivance. The point here is that *if* such a remarkable event were to transpire, *I* for one should certainly be convinced that God does exist."

Doesn't Hanson have a point? God could make it a lot easier for everyone to believe in him, couldn't he? Sometimes it seems that God keeps himself so well hidden that it's hard even to believe he exists. Why doesn't God silence all scoffers by making a public appearance?

Where Is Your God?

The hiddenness of God isn't a problem just for atheists. The prophet Isaiah was no atheist, but he still wished God would do more to show himself and demonstrate his power. Isaiah prayed, "Oh, that you would rend the heavens and come down, that the mountains would tremble before you! ...Come down to make your name known to your enemies and cause the nations to quake before you" (Isaiah 64:1-2). When Isaiah said this, the Lord had been keeping a low profile. It was hard for God's people to trust him and easy for God's enemies to ignore him. Isaiah wanted God to come out of hiding and unleash his power for all to see. Isaiah wanted the Lord to do pretty much what N. R. Hanson suggested.

Sometimes, even when you know God exists, he still doesn't feel very near, and his ways don't seem very clear. You wish he would do something dramatic not only to silence unbelievers but also to encourage believers. Many believers go through spiritual dry spells. Maybe you know what that is like. You believe in God, but you don't really sense his presence, and your heart feels empty and dry. That's how David felt when he wrote in Psalm 42, "As the deer pants for streams of water, so my soul pants for you, O God. My soul thirsts for God, for the living God. When can I go and meet with God? My tears have been my food day and night, while men say to me all day long, 'Where is your God?'" It's hard when you're panting for God, and he's nowhere to be found.

The problem becomes even more intense when you're feeling crushed by hardships and pain, and God remains hidden. You call on the Lord, you pray to him with all your might, but nothing happens. The cancer keeps advancing, or the marriage keeps crumbling, or society keeps going downhill. You keep praying, but God keeps hiding, and the only answer you get is silence.

You might find yourself wondering along with a biblical psalm writer, "Why, O Lord, do you stand far off? Why do you hide yourself in times of trouble?" (Psalm 10:1).

Good question! Why does God hide when it seems we need him most? Why doesn't an atheist get a revelation of God that he simply can't deny? Why doesn't a Christian going through a spiritual dry spell always get a supernatural experience to refresh her spirits? When people in trouble pray and pray, why doesn't God give them a miracle or at least an explanation? Why is it so hard to see God at work in the events around us? Isaiah says, "Truly you are a God who hides himself" (Isaiah 45:15). Why is that? What possible reasons could God have for hiding himself?

Seeing His Face

You might think that if God exists, he should show his face and remove all possibility of doubt. That's what you'd do if you were God! But be careful what you ask for. When you demand to see God's face, you may end up with more than you bargained for.

According to the Bible, the day is coming when the Lord won't hide any longer. He's going to do exactly what unbelievers say he should do if he's really God. Jesus is going to crack open the skies, he's going to shake the earth, and he's going to make a public, earth-shattering appearance that will leave no room for doubt. He will show himself, and everyone will see his face. However, the moment the Lord does that, it will be too late for those who don't already belong to him. Listen to this vision from Revelation 6:

There was a great earthquake... The sky receded like a scroll, rolling up, and every mountain and island was removed from its place.

Then the kings of the earth, the princes, the generals, the rich, the mighty, and every slave and every free man hid in caves and among the rocks of the mountains. They called to the mountains and rocks, "Fall on us and hide us from the face of him who sits on the throne and from the wrath of the Lamb! For the great day of their wrath has come, and who can stand?" (v.12,14-17)

These people would rather be buried in a landslide than stand in God's awful presence. His face is an unbearable terror to them. When the Lord stops hiding himself, they will try to hide themselves. They will find his majesty and purity unbearable.

If you say you won't believe in God unless he shows himself openly, watch out! If God met your demand, you wouldn't just calmly change your mind and say, "Now I've got my proof. I guess God exists after all." No, you'd be terrorized and repelled by the awesome splendor of God, and you'd be lost forever.

The Bible says that God hides himself and delays the public return of Christ because "he is patient with you, not wanting anyone to perish, but everyone to come to repentance" (2 Peter 3:9). When God hides himself, he leaves room for doubt, but he also leaves room for repentance. When God stops hiding, there will no longer be room for either. The Lord's face will have an eternal and overwhelming attraction for those who have learned to love him in his hiddenness, but his face will have the opposite effect for all others. His irresistible holiness will repel them and send them hurtling away from him into hell.

So don't be too quick to demand the kind of encounter with God that will occur only at Jesus' second coming. First, make sure you've accepted the Lord in his first coming. Jesus came as a humble man, rather than in divine glory. The Lord hid himself in humility in order to reveal himself in a form that would save us rather than destroy us. God's hiddenness may sometimes be a source of frustration, but don't forget: it's also the source of salvation. At one level, then, we can say that God hides himself because he is patient and merciful with sinners. He's giving more time to repent and prepare to meet him face to face.

Why Not More Miracles?

Still, you might wonder, even if God hides his face in order to spare us, couldn't he make himself a bit more obvious? He wouldn't have to show himself directly; he could just do a few supernatural things now and then to prove he's alive and well. Why doesn't God do more miracles to impress us?

Well, God *has* done some amazing miracles. He parted the Red Sea for Moses; he toppled the walls of Jericho for Joshua; he sent fire from heaven at Elijah's request. But even if we believe these amazing stories in the Bible, they don't really solve our problem. We haven't seen the sea parted lately or walls tumbling or fire from heaven to prove unbelievers wrong.

Jesus himself performed many miracles during his time on earth, but today we don't see miracles on the scale of Jesus' miracles. Oh, there may be an occasional reduction of arthritis pain, or an unexpected recovery from cancer, or an amazing occurrence once in a while—but miracles like Jesus performed? When was the last time you saw someone blind from birth given his sight, or 5,000 people fed out of one lunch box, or a man walking on water, or a dead person raised to life again? Even if the Lord hides his face in order to spare us, why doesn't he at least show more of his hand and reveal himself through miracles as mighty as those in the Bible?

That's a tough question, and I don't have an easy answer. In some ways the answer is as hidden as God himself. But here are a few things to keep in mind.

One is that God is the Creator and sustainer of everything that exists. He's constantly at work, even when he's not doing what we might label "miracles." The ordinary workings of creation are God's work just as much as the extraordinary working of miracles. Without the eyes of faith, we may think God is doing nothing, when in fact he's upholding everything.

Another fact to remember is that God is free. He can do miracles whenever he pleases, and he can refrain from doing miracles whenever he pleases. He can say "yes" to our prayers for a miracle, and he can say "no." He's God; we're not. He's free to do as he pleases.

Still another thing to remember is that miracles don't have a very good track record of changing people's hearts. If you don't love God already, you're not going to start loving him just because he gives a supernatural demonstration. When God sent ten supernatural plagues on Egypt, Pharaoh simply became more stubborn with every one. When God gave the Israelites manna in the wilderness, they grumbled more than ever. When Elijah called down fire from heaven to demonstrate God's power, Queen Jezebel tried all the harder to kill Elijah. And when Jesus did his miracles, his opponents either tried to explain them away or else credited them to the power of Satan. Eventually they seized Jesus and crucified him.

God's Hiding Place

Jesus' supreme achievement didn't occur in any of his miracles but in his death. His miracles didn't remove anyone's sin; only his death could take away the sin of the world. The ultimate revelation of God's glory didn't occur in impressive miracles but in the disgrace of the cross. Nowhere was God more hidden in deeper darkness and nowhere was he more clearly revealed than at the cross. So if we look for God only in miracles, we may never find him at all; but if we look for God at the cross of Christ, we'll find him every time.

We tend to have our own ideas of where we should be able to find God and what God ought to be like. We imagine that God ought to do what we would do if we were God. If we were God, we'd use our power every chance we got. We'd show off a little. But the Lord often prefers weakness to power. If we were in charge of the world, we'd grind our enemies into the dirt and give our friends every miracle they ever wanted. But the Lord is often kind to his enemies and puts his friends through difficult trials.

If we had been in Jesus' shoes—a ridiculous thought, since we're so unlike Christ—but if we had been in Jesus' shoes, we'd have taken every opportunity to prove who we were. But Jesus often preferred to hide himself. Even when he did miracles for people, he often instructed them to tell no one. And he always refused to do miracles when his opponents demanded supernatural signs. Even when he was being tortured, Jesus refused to use his divine power. Some mockers laughed at him and called for him to come down from the cross if he were really their Messiah, but Jesus took the abuse and kept hanging there. Is that what you or I would have done if we had the power to rescue ourselves? We wouldn't have kept suffering. We'd have saved ourselves and put the hurt on our enemies. But Jesus stayed on the cross and kept suffering until he died.

Even after his resurrection, the Lord didn't do what you or I would have done. He appeared only to certain select witnesses before he returned to heaven. Everybody watched Jesus die, but fewer saw him after his resurrection. In Jesus' place, we'd have made a grand appearance to the entire city of Jerusalem and said, "I told you so!" Instead, Jesus appeared to some people who loved him—a few hundred in all—and then returned to heaven. Everybody else would simply have to take their word for it that Jesus was alive.

You and I would not have handled things the way Jesus did. That's one more proof that God is God and we're not. He's not like us. He isn't like we imagine him to be. He doesn't do what we expect him to do. "For my thoughts are not your thoughts, neither are your ways my ways," declares the Lord. "As the heavens are higher than the earth, so are my ways higher than your ways, and my thoughts than your thoughts" (Isaiah 55:8-9).

The Lord doesn't consult us when he's deciding what to do. He does things his way, in his time, for his purposes. As the apostle Paul explained, religious people demand miracles, and educated people want wisdom, but the gospel message is Christ crucified. That sounds offensive to miracle-lovers and crazy to intellectuals, but to those who are being saved, Christ crucified is God's power and wisdom (1 Cor. 1:18-25).

If you want to find the God who hides, you can't just look where you'd expect him to be, based on what you would do if you were God. You need to seek God as he really is, and you need to know where he's hiding. He's not hiding in a logical proof or a sensational miracle. His favorite hiding place is in the message of the cross. That's where you'll find him.

Here we see another reason God hides himself: he wants to humble us. The way of God is the way of the cross, and the way of the cross is the way of humility. The cross humbles us by showing that we're sinners in need of Jesus' sacrifice, and it humbles us by ignoring our demands for supernatural signs and logical proofs and showing us that our qualifications don't count for much. The Lord is God, and we're not. We have to depend on him completely for our salvation and for everything else. Only then are we ready to know him at all. Only then can we meet him face to face.

Why Must Believers Struggle?

But what if you're already a Christian? Why would God hide from you? You've trusted in Jesus' death and resurrection, you've trusted the Holy Spirit to fill you and lead you, and yet you may still have times when God seems distant and far away. Your soul is dry. Your heart feels empty. You're going through a spiritual drought, and God is hiding.

Or maybe you're facing a terrible tragedy or hardship. Awful things have been happening, and God hasn't done much to improve the situation in spite of all your prayers. Why not? Why would God hide himself even from someone who already belongs to him?

Again, I don't have easy answers, but let's look at this from the opposite angle. What would happen if you felt close to God 24 hours a day, if you always understood everything he was doing in your life, if you never found anything in the Bible puzzling, if all your prayers were answered with a "yes," and if God gave you all kinds of supernatural abilities? Sounds like heaven on earth, doesn't it? But what would really happen?

The Bible gives an example. The church in the city of Corinth was one where God gave people great insights and miracles and supernatural powers. But this church, with all its knowledge and blessings, turned out to be terribly unspiritual. They were so proud of what they knew that they became know-it-alls. They became so satisfied with miracles and supernatural experiences that some of them even thought the resurrection wouldn't be necessary. They thought they already had it all; they didn't need anything more.

What happened in Corinth shows what can happen to us if God pours too many good things on immature Christians who still have many sins and weaknesses. If we know too much, it can make us proud. If we're blessed too much, it can make us complacent. We know something of God, and if we're not careful, we start to think we know it all. We think we can figure him out for ourselves. We think we're experts on God. We become proud that God is our pal, that we know him up close and personal, and a lot of other people don't. Knowledge can lead to pride, and blessings can lead to complacency. If our lives were one spiritual high after another, one answer to prayer after another, if God made everything go just the way we wanted, we might get so satisfied with life here and now that we wouldn't long for Jesus to come again and make all things new. Who needs the second coming or the final resurrection? We've already got it all! But if we're less comfortable and less complacent, we're more eager for Jesus to return and more eager for the new creation.

Humble and Hungry

That may be part of the reason God hides himself even from Christians, why he allows us to go through spiritual dry spells, why he sometimes sends trials instead of blessings. God hides himself to make us humble, and he hides himself to make us hungry. He makes us humble by showing us how little we know him or understand his ways, and he makes us hungry for heaven by letting us feel the pain and brokenness of this present world.

Right now, we're still a long way from heaven. We see dimly; only later will we see face to face. We walk by faith, not by sight. We must not only trust in Christ crucified, but we must walk the way of the cross ourselves. This doesn't mean we should stop longing for heaven. It just means we realize we're not there yet. It doesn't mean we stop longing for a richer relationship with God; it just means we realize how far we have to go.

Paul wrote, "Knowledge puffs up, but love builds up. The man who thinks he knows something does not yet know as he ought to know. But the man who loves God is known by God" (1 Corinthians 8:1-3). One of the most important things you can know about God is that no matter how well you think you know him, you still don't know him very well. What matters is that he knows you, and that he's moving you to love him.

Isaiah cried, "Truly you are a God who hides himself, O God and Savior of Israel... But Israel will be saved by the Lord with an everlasting salvation; you will never be put to shame or disgraced." Just a few verses later, this God who hides himself says, "I have not spoken in secret, from somewhere in a land of darkness; I have not said, 'Seek me in vain'" (Isaiah 45:15-19). It's hide and seek: God hides so that we will seek him, for only the seeking heart, the heart that is humble and hungry for God, can ever be ready to know God as he truly is.

Sometimes God teaches us more by making us ask hard questions than by giving us easy answers. He shows as much about himself by what he hides as by what he reveals. The Lord shows enough of himself in Christ and in Scripture to give us faith and hope and love, and at the same time he conceals himself enough to make us humble and to make us hunger all the more for the day when we see him face to face and he makes all things new.

Chapter 15

Where is God When We Suffer?

Ted Turner was twenty years old when he stopped believing in God. Turner is famous for his billions of dollars, his vast media empire, and his professional sports teams. What perhaps isn't so well known is that during his youth, Ted Turner considered himself a Christian. At age seventeen he even thought about becoming a missionary. But by the time Ted was twenty, he refused to believe in God any longer.

What happened? When Ted was twenty, his seventeen-year-old sister Mary Jane died. Her death came after five years of suffering from a horrible disease. As Ted watched Mary Jane suffer and finally die, in spite of many prayers for healing, he decided that there was no God. How could such a thing happen if an all-powerful and loving God was in control of the universe?

I have something in common with Ted Turner. I've watched the horrible suffering of someone I loved. My wife and I had a baby who suffered in the hospital for more than five months, and it seemed God did nothing to help that little girl. Rebekah went through the painful process of having a respirator inserted down her throat at least nine different times during her illness. She endured several surgeries. She received so many medications and feedings through intravenous needles that after a while the nurses had a hard time finding a new vein that would work for the next intravenous. Sometimes they would spend more than an hour jabbing a needle into Rebekah's wrists and ankles and scalp before they could get a suitable vein. For nearly half a year she suffered such things, and then she died.

Where was God during all this? Where was God while baby Rebekah was crying and bleeding and gasping for breath? Where was God when Ted Turner's sister wasted away and died? Ted believes that God was nowhere—he doesn't exist. I, on the other hand, believe in God. I believe that he is perfectly good and that he is all-powerful. I don't know all the answers about my daughter's illness and death, and I certainly don't claim to have an explanation for the pain and tragedy of so many others. But I still believe in God.

Almost everyone, at one time or another, has to face the question, "Where is God when we suffer?" An encounter with pain and grief changes a person's relationship to God. When your mind is reeling and your heart is aching, something happens. You either fall into God's arms, or else you fall away from him. It all depends on whether you know God as he really is.

If you think of God only as the supreme Ruler of the universe who sits in his plush throne room in heaven, maintains a safe distance from your suffering, and refuses to do anything about it, then it will be very hard not to join Ted Turner. You may either stop believing in God altogether, or else hate him for permitting such terrible pain to afflict you and those you love.

However, if you know God as he really is, as he is revealed at the cross of Jesus, you will keep trusting him no matter what, even when you endure pain you can't escape and struggle with questions you can't answer. Whatever else may be true of God, he doesn't just sit in some heavenly control room, oblivious to your suffering. If you know the Christ of the cross, you know that God loves you, that he understands your suffering, and that he will never let you go.

Throughout history, philosophers have looked at the pain and tragedy in the world and asked, "Is it logically possible for God to exist in a world that includes such dreadful suffering?" Some argue that a perfectly good God would *want* to prevent suffering, and that an all-powerful God would *be able* to prevent it. Therefore, goes the reasoning, if God existed, suffering would not exist. But since suffering obviously does exist, God does not.

That's an interesting, challenging problem for philosophers, and having earned a degree in philosophy, I've studied it carefully. Christian philosophers have suggested reasonable answers to this intellectual puzzle. Some of their answers are quite convincing, but I'm not going to go into them here. Instead, I want to speak to people who are actually suffering, not just those who debate suffering as an abstract question. I've found that abstract answers to an intellectual puzzle aren't very helpful during the actual experience of suffering. It was one thing for me to be a philosophy major analyzing the problem of suffering; it was quite another to be a father, watching my own child die.

Logic really isn't the issue when you come face to face with anguish. When you're going through terrible times, or when someone you love is caught in the grip of Alzheimer's disease, or wasting away from cancer, or killed by a drunk driver, you don't simply need a logical proof that God exists. You want to know, "Where is God when we suffer, and what is he doing?"

The Bible shows us at least four ways that God is involved in the suffering of his people: First, he *shares* in our suffering. Second, he is *sovereign* over our suffering. Third, he *sustains* us during our suffering. And fourth, he *saves* us from suffering.

God Shares in Our Suffering

Some people seem to have the idea that God is far removed from our pain. To them God is like a general who keeps sending troops to the front line with no concern for how many casualties there are. He doesn't care how much his troops have to suffer as long as they accomplish his objectives. He himself is protected from any pain or danger in his safe, comfortable headquarters.

The author of a brief drama called "The Long Silence" forces us to take another look at how we think about God.

At the end of time, billions of people were scattered on a great plain before God's throne.

Most shrank back from the brilliant light before them. But some groups near the front talked heatedly— not with cringing shame, but with belligerence.

"Can God judge us? How can he know about suffering?" snapped a pert young brunette. She ripped open a sleeve to reveal a tattooed number from a Nazi concentration camp. "We endured terror ... beatings ... torture ... death!"

In another group a boy lowered his collar. "What about this?" he demanded, showing an ugly rope burn. "Lynched ... for no crime but being black!"

In another crowd there was a pregnant schoolgirl with sullen eyes. "Why should I suffer?" she murmured, "It wasn't my fault."

Far out across the plain there were hundreds of such groups. Each had a complaint against God for the evil and suffering he permitted in his world. How lucky God was to live in heaven where all was sweetness and light, where there was no weeping or fear, no hunger or hatred. What did God know of all that man had been forced to endure in this world? For God leads a pretty sheltered life, they said.

So each of these groups sent forth their leader, chosen because he had suffered the most... In the center of the plain they consulted with each other. At last they were ready to present their case. It was rather clever.

Before God could be qualified to be their judge, he must endure what they had endured. Their decision was that God should be sentenced to live on earth—as a man!

"Let him be born a Jew. Let the legitimacy of his birth be doubted. Give him a work so difficult that even his family will think him out of his mind when he tries to do it. Let him be betrayed by his closest friends. Let him face false charges, be tried by a prejudiced jury and convicted by a cowardly judge. Let him be tortured.

"At the last, let him see what it means to be terribly alone. Then let him die. Let him die so that there can be no doubt that he died. Let there be a great host of witnesses to verify it."

As each leader announced his portion of the sentence, loud murmurs of approval went up from the throng of people assembled.

And when the last had finished pronouncing sentence, there was a long silence. No one uttered another word. No one moved. For suddenly all knew that God had already served his sentence.

Whatever we don't understand about God, one thing we can never say is that God has no idea what it's like to suffer. At the cross we discover a God whose suffering goes beyond anything we can imagine. Jesus suffered the horrors of hell. He felt completely abandoned by his Father in heaven. He cried out, "My God, my God, why have you forsaken me?" (Matthew 27:46).

Even before Jesus came to earth and took the world's pain upon himself, God shared in the suffering of his people. For example, after describing the oppression that God's people were enduring because of their sin, Judges 10:16 says, "The Lord could bear Israel's misery no longer." Their pain was his pain, and he couldn't stand it any more! Or look at Isaiah 63:9, "In all their distress, he too was distressed." When God's people suffer, he suffers with them.

It was true in Old Testament times, it was supremely true at the cross, and it is true throughout the New Testament age to this very day: The Lord suffers with his people. Saul of Tarsus, later to become the apostle Paul, was going around tormenting and killing Christians until one day Jesus appeared to him in blazing light and said, "I am Jesus, whom you are persecuting." When Jesus' followers were being persecuted, Jesus himself was being persecuted. He felt their suffering and called it his own.

The fact that the Lord continues to identify with the suffering of his people is also clear in one of Jesus' parables about the last judgment. Jesus will say, "I was hungry, I was thirsty, I was a stranger, I needed clothes, I was sick, I was in prison" (Matthew 25:31-46). And when does all this happen to Jesus? Whenever it happens to the least of his people. Where is God when his people suffer? The Lord is there suffering too.

God is Sovereign Over Suffering

The Bible doesn't just say that God shares in our suffering; it also shows that he is sovereign over our suffering. The word "sovereign" simply means that God is always in charge. No event, no matter how shocking or painful, catches God by surprise. God is in control, and he can take even the most tragic circumstances and use them to advance his plans for our good.

Some people seem to think that most of what's wrong with the world is beyond God's control. God is very kind, and it hurts him to see us suffer, they think, but sometimes he can't do very much about it. God is as frustrated and outraged about the situation as anyone, but he lacks the power to change it.

One noted thinker, Elie Wiesel, responded to this picture of God by saying, "If that's who God is, why doesn't he resign and let someone more competent take his place?"

According to the Bible, whatever the reason for suffering may be, it is not because God is too weak to prevent it. God is sovereign over all things, including suffering. He is in control even in the most horrifying circumstances. The cross proves it.

Jesus did not die because God was helpless to prevent his death. Jesus was handed over to be crucified "by God's set purpose and foreknowledge" (Acts 2:23). When Jesus' enemies tortured and killed him, they were doing what God's "power and will had decided beforehand should happen" (Acts 4:28). God was in control, and Jesus accepted the path of suffering, knowing that God was sovereign. In his sovereignty, God used the most horrible injustice the world has ever known, the crucifixion of his own Son, to bring the world salvation.

Now, if God was in control even at the cross, and if, from something so horrible, he could bring about the salvation of the world, we can be certain that he is also sovereign over our suffering. In light of the cross, we can declare, "We know that in all things God works for the good of those who love him, who have been called according to his purpose" (Romans 8:28). This doesn't mean we should pretend to enjoy our suffering, or think that God is the direct cause of all of it, but we can expect God to use even the worst things to bring about something good. We may not always know or understand what God's purpose is, but we can be sure that he is in control at every moment. God is sovereign even over suffering, and he will use it to serve his purpose in the lives of his people.

God Sustains Us During Our Suffering

Where is God when we suffer? He shares in our suffering; he is sovereign over our suffering; and he sustains us during our suffering. God promises that he will sustain, support, and carry his people through hard times. God says, "I have upheld you since you were conceived, and have carried you since your birth. Even to your old age and gray hairs I am he, I am he who will sustain you. I have made you, and I will carry you. I will sustain you, and I will rescue you (Isaiah 46:3-4).

You may be familiar with a little story called "Footprints." It's not in the Bible, but the point it makes is true to the Bible.

One night a man had a dream. He was walking along the beach with the Lord. Across the sky flashed scenes from his life. For each scene he noticed two sets of footprints in the sand: one set belonged to him, the other to the Lord.

Looking back at the footprints, he noticed that at many times during his life, there was just one set of footprints. He also noticed that this always happened at the lowest, saddest times of his life.

This bothered him greatly, so he spoke to Jesus about it: "Lord, you said that if I gave my life to you, you would walk with me all the way. But I see that at the hardest times in my life, when I needed you most, you left me to walk alone."

The Savior replied, "My precious child, I would never leave you. In those terrible times where you see one set of footprints—it was then that I carried you."

"The eternal God is your refuge, and underneath are the everlasting arms" (Deuteronomy 33:27). The Lord says, "I will never leave you nor forsake you" (Hebrews 13:5). Even when we walk through the valley of the shadow of death, we don't have to be afraid, for he is with us (Psalm 23:4). Because Jesus himself endured being forsaken by his heavenly Father, those who trust in Jesus will never be forsaken by God. The Lord is there to support us and carry us. Even when we seem utterly abandoned, God's loving grace is sufficient to sustain us.

God Saves Us From Suffering

Where is God when we suffer? He shares our suffering; he is sovereign over our suffering; he sustains us through our suffering; and last but not least, he saves us from suffering. Here again the cross of Jesus is the focus of our hope. "Let us fix our eyes on Jesus, the author and perfecter of our faith, who for the joy set before him endured the cross, scorning its shame, and sat down at the right hand of the throne of God" (Hebrews 12:2). Jesus endured the cross for the joy set before him; he knew he would win in the end. His suffering soon gave way to the glory of the resurrection. Jesus rose to life in his glorious, immortal body, and someday all his people, and indeed the whole creation, will share in his victory over suffering and death. "They will be his people, and God himself will be with them and be their God. He will wipe every tear from their eyes. There will be no more death or mourning or crying or pain, for the old order of things has passed away" (Revelation 1:3-4). "Everlasting joy will crown their heads. Gladness and joy will overtake them, and sorrow and sighing will flee away" (Isaiah 51:11).

This great hope of eternal happiness helped me to deal with the pain and confusion when my daughter died. At first I couldn't help thinking to myself, "From the moment Rebekah was born until she died more than five months later, almost all she did was suffer. What did she do to deserve that?" But then I asked myself another question: "Rebekah is now living in perfect happiness in the glorious presence of Jesus, not just for five months, but for all eternity. What did she do to deserve that?"

When we trust in Jesus, when we fix our minds on him and on the joy of eternal life, our painful questions are overwhelmed by wonder. We might not be able to answer all our questions about suffering, but we can say, "I consider that our present sufferings are not worth comparing with the glory that will be revealed in us" (Romans 8:18). We believe in a God who saves us from suffering, and his salvation leads to a future so glorious that none of our sufferings now are worth comparing to it.

So where is God when his people suffer? He shares our suffering; he is sovereign over our suffering; he sustains us during our suffering; and he saves us from our suffering. These four great truths don't answer all our questions. We might not know the exact reason for our suffering; we might not know how long it will continue; but whatever we don't know, we know enough to be sure that God is worthy of our confidence. Even when we don't understand everything, we understand enough to know that at the cross of Jesus, we are meeting a God we can trust. The God of the cross is a God you can believe in, no matter what.

> If we have never sought, we seek thee now;
> Thine eyes burn through the dark, our only stars;
> We must have sight of thorn marks on thy brow,
> We must have thee, O Jesus of the scars.
> The heavens frighten us, they are too calm;
> In all the universe we have no place.
> Our wounds are hurting us; where is the balm?
> Lord Jesus, by thy scars we know thy grace.
> The other gods were strong; but thou wast weak;
> They rode, but thou didst stumble to a throne;
> But to our wounds only God's wounds can speak,
> And not a god has wounds, but thou alone.
>
> (Edward Shillito)

Chapter 16

Hijacking the Truth

Once upon a time there was a man who woke up with a hangover after a night of heavy drinking. When the alarm clock went off, his brain almost exploded. He buried his face deeper into his pillow and groaned something that sounded like "crawl the octopus." His wife had heard this before and knew it meant, "Call the office." So she called the place where her husband worked and left a message saying he was sick and couldn't make it. At the breakfast table she repeated the story to her children: Daddy was sick and wouldn't be eating with them. She then drove the kids to school and headed off to work herself.

About noon the drunkard finally woke up again and dragged himself out of bed. He staggered to the place where he kept his liquor and spent most of the afternoon drinking. Then he went out into the backyard. That's when he saw the roses.

There was a thriving rosebush out behind the house, and a number of lovely, red roses were blossoming. When he saw the roses, he got an idea. "I'll show my wife what a good husband I am. I'll surprise her with a bunch of fresh-cut roses. I may not be a perfect husband," he told himself, "but she could do worse. She's gonna love these flowers!"

He hurried back into the house and got a sharp knife out of the kitchen drawer. On his way back out the door, he grabbed a bottle and took a few extra swallows to keep his strength up for the task ahead of him.

When he reached the rosebush, he grabbed one of the stems. Immediately he jerked his hand away. Blood was seeping in several places where thorns had pierced the skin. He hesitated a moment, then grabbed the stem again. The thorns jabbed him again, but he hung on. He hacked away at the stem until finally it came free in his hand. He tossed it aside and grabbed another, again drawing blood. Thanks to the alcohol, however, the thorns didn't hurt much.

He kept at it for several minutes and was just cutting the last stem when he heard a car pull into the driveway. His wife and children were back. Hurriedly he gathered the roses in his arms, scratching and pricking his arms and chest. Then he took one last swallow from the bottle and strutted back into the house to give his wife and children a wonderful surprise.

He thrust the roses at the startled children and said, "Hey, kids, look what I got for your ma!" Then he swept them into his arms, squeezing them along with the roses.

"Ouch!" the children squealed as the sharp thorns poked their skin. "Let go, Dad! You're hurting us!"

"Whassa matter?" cried the drunk. "Don'tcha love your dear ol' dad? C'mon! Gimme a hug!" As they tried to squirm loose, he squeezed the children all the harder and drove the thorns deeper.

They screamed some more, until finally he let them go and turned toward his wife. He waved the roses in her face and asked, "Waddaya think, honey? Purty nice, huh?" He stepped toward her but tripped and fell against her. The thorny stems scratched her face and poked her neck. She gasped in pain and pushed him away.

"Get away from me!" she shouted. "You've been drinking again, haven't you? This is the night we're supposed to go to a ball game as a family, and here you are, drunk again."

The drunkard's sloppy grin turned to a scowl. "I'm not drunk," he grumped. "I just had a little pick-me-up. I slave away getting flowers for you, and this is the thanks I get! C'mon," he said, thrusting the thorny bundle into her face once more. "Give 'em a sniff. Nice, huh? You know, 'A rose by any other name would smell as sweet.' 'A rose is a rose is a rose...'"

"You fool," his wife shrieked, jerking her face away in pain. "Don't talk to me about roses. If you want to quote fancy sayings, try this: 'A drunk is a drunk is a drunk.' Or how about this: 'A drunk by any other name would smell as bad.'"

That's not a very uplifting story, is it? Well, it's just a story I made up—though similar things do happen. I tell you this story to bring to life a word picture in the Bible: "Like a thornbush in a drunkard's hand is a proverb in the mouth of a fool" (Proverbs 26:9). Can you picture it? A drunk staggers around waving a bunch of thorny branches, thinking he's great, but hurting himself and those close to him. That is what it's like when a fool goes around quoting wise sayings. He does more harm than good.

Dangerous Bible

Sharp insights become dangerous when the wrong person is using them. This is true even of the Bible itself. God's Book is perfect in every way, but it can still do a lot of damage—not because anything is wrong with the Bible, but because something is wrong with some people who quote the Bible. Just as roses are lovely except when a drunk is waving them around, so the Bible is wonderful except when a fool is waving it around.

Maybe you know what it's like to be wounded by someone who hurts you and then makes it worse by quoting Bible verses to you. Or maybe you are guilty of this yourself: you misuse the Bible in a way that harms other people and yourself as well. This is more common than we'd like to think. Some drunkards use Bible verses about wine to defend their drinking. Some men hit their wives and then quote Bible verses about submission. Some parents abuse their children and quote verses about children honoring parents. Nasty critics cut others down and then quote biblical proverbs about how good and helpful a rebuke can be. Perverted people break every command in the Bible, but the moment anyone challenges their behavior, they quote the words of Jesus, "Judge not, that you be not judged." The list goes on and on. For almost every statement in the Bible, there's a fool somewhere who can find a way to misuse and abuse it.

The results are so devastating that we can't begin to measure the damage. We can't begin to count all the people who walk away from the church because of parents or church leaders or other hypocrites who quote the Bible even as they commit horrible sins. We can't begin to count all the people who not only hurt others but destroy themselves by quoting Scripture as an excuse for sin. We can't begin to imagine how it grieves and angers God to see the holy words of his Book misused to cause so much harm and pain.

Some folks blame the Bible for the way in which people misuse it. But is the Bible to blame? Would you say that roses are bad just because some drunkard is waving them around and hurting himself and other people? Or that God is bad for creating roses? Of course not. So we shouldn't blame the Bible, either, for the way foolish people have misused it. Instead, we should ask how we can understand the Bible rightly and use it properly as God intends.

The Bible can be dangerous, but is that because it is full of lies? No, it's because the Bible is full of truth. Lies can be dangerous, but truth can be even more dangerous. The more certain a truth is, and the higher the authority that stands behind it, the more dangerous it becomes when we misuse it. That makes the Bible the most dangerous book there is, because it is backed by the authority of God himself. It speaks with such authority and its truths are so powerful that when we misuse those truths to serve our own preferences and prejudices, we can do horrid things and feel confident that we have the full support of God himself.

I've already said that drunkards, wife beaters, slanderers, and perverts can twist Bible verses to suit their own evils. In addition to these and other individual sins, I could mention a number of large-scale social sins that have been committed by Bible-quoters. How many people have died in religious wars, or suffered a slave driver's whip, or endured horrible discrimination and cruelty from groups of people marching under a cross and quoting the Bible?

When you see all the damage that can be done by religious, Bible-quoting people, you may be tempted to reject the Bible.

You may be tempted to reject any notion of absolute truth altogether. You figure that it would be better to see everything as just a matter of opinion. If nobody would believe in such a thing as absolute truth, then nobody could use it against others. If there were no binding moral standards, maybe we could all just get along and respect each other. A growing number of people seem to feel that the only solution to the misuse of truth is to explode the idea that there is any such thing as absolute truth.

But that's like trying to prevent the hijacking of airplanes by blowing up all airplanes. Sure, it's terrible when someone hijacks an airplane, but don't blame the airplane. Blame the hijacker. Don't destroy all airplanes. Guard against hijacking.

That's what we need to do when we face the fact that truth can be hijacked and used to harm others or hold them hostage. Don't blame the truth; blame the person who is hijacking the truth. Don't deny the truth of the Bible; instead, try to help those who have been hurt by the misuse of the Bible, and then try to guard against the misuse of biblical truth in the future.

Besides, you can't destroy the truth even if you want to. Truth is truth no matter what. You can deny it and ignore it, but you can't destroy it. The Word of God stands forever. You might as well face the fact that the Bible is true from cover to cover and get on with finding out what it takes to use God's Word rightly instead of wrongly.

Five Principles

Here are five basic principles for using the Bible in a healthy way. All five are connected.

The first is this: *Get right with God*. When you read the Bible, you won't get its message right unless you are right with the God who authored the Bible. To grasp the truth, it's not enough to have truth speak to you from the outside. You need truth on the inside. A prayer in the Bible says, "Surely I was sinful at birth... Surely you desire truth in the inner parts; you teach me wisdom in the inmost place... Create in me a pure heart, O God, and renew a steadfast spirit within me" (Psalm 51:5-10).

To get right with God, you need to be changed on the inside. The Bible says, "As a dog returns to its vomit, so a fool repeats his folly" (Proverbs 26:11). A dog can't help acting like a dog, and a sinful fool can't help acting like a sinful fool. He needs to become a new person. But for that to happen, he first needs to realize how much he needs to change. The very next verse after the one about the dog and his vomit says, "Do you see a man wise in his own eyes? There is more hope for a fool than for him" (Proverbs 26:12).

Think again of a drunkard waving roses. He thinks he's wise and charming, but he's hurting himself and his family. His outer problems result from an inner problem: he's drunk. And because he's drunk, he doesn't really know what he's doing. He can't think straight or control himself properly. In order for him to behave properly, he first needs to get sober and realize how foolish he's been. He needs to change inside.

That's not just true of drunkards. It's true of us all. We need to be made right on the inside. We need God's Holy Spirit to give us a new spirit and heart. We need to get right with God.

Here's a second principle for making right use of biblical truth: *Listen to the whole Bible.* Don't just focus on a verse here or there. God's truth isn't a collection of isolated sayings. It is a unity. The moment we isolate one part of the Bible's teaching from the rest, we distort it and misunderstand its true meaning.

For example, the Bible says that children need discipline and punishment—perhaps even physical punishment in some cases. The child abuser focuses on this truth as he beats his children. But he conveniently ignores Bible passages which show that discipline must be applied in love and only with great restraint. A verse like Colossians 3:21, "Fathers, do not embitter your children, or they will become discouraged" goes in one ear and out the other.

Here's another example of listening to some biblical statements and ignoring others. The Bible says wonderful things about God's love. But if you take only those statements about love and ignore parts of the Bible which speak about God's wrath, you end up with a sugary view of God. You don't take his warnings of judgment seriously, and you don't really have a clue why Jesus had to die. Only when you take seriously the statements about God's wrath will see you that Jesus died to suffer God's punishment against your sin, and only then will you repent of your sins and trust in Jesus alone for your salvation.

That brings us to the third and central thing to keep in mind as we read the Bible: *Focus on Jesus.* I've just pointed out that we need to see God's truth as a unity, not as a bunch of isolated fragments. But why is the truth a unity? Because all the truths of the Bible form a personal unity in the Lord Jesus Christ. Everything we learn in the Bible is intended by God to draw us closer to Christ and to make us more like him.

You need to focus on Jesus in order for the Bible's truth to come into focus. You'll misread and misuse what the Bible says unless you see it in relationship to Christ. Jesus once told some religious leaders that all their Bible study was useless because they refused to see that the Scriptures were pointing to him (John 5:39-40). Everything in the Bible is there to fill your heart with faith in Jesus, fill your minds with thoughts of Jesus, and fill your life with the character of Jesus.

In fact, as you read the Bible, hear it as the voice of Jesus, and talk with Jesus while he talks to you. Make your Bible reading a dialogue with Jesus, listening to him and praying to him, seeking to stay in touch with Jesus and in tune with him.

A fourth principle for healthy use of the Bible is this: *Apply it to yourself personally.* Don't use the Bible only as a weapon against other people. Some of the worst misuses of the Bible come when you are so busy applying it to someone else that you miss what it says to you.

Why do some husbands know exactly what the Bible says to their wives about submission, and pay so little attention to what it says to husbands about love and self-sacrifice? Why do some sharp-tongued wives lecture their husbands on what the Bible tells husbands to do but ignore Proverbs 27:15, "A quarrelsome wife is like a constant dripping on a rainy day"?

Why do people with a good job and plenty of money quote Bible passages to the poor about laziness causing poverty and ignore passages which warn the rich against exploiting others and refusing to share with others? Why do some people who are indeed lazy and abuse the welfare system quote Bible verses about helping the poor and ignore statements like, "If a man will not work, he shall not eat" (2 Thessalonians 3:10)?

Most of us act like experts on the sins of others rather than first dealing with our own sins. Jesus says, "How can you say to your brother, 'Let me take the speck out of your eye,' when all the time there is a plank in your own? You hypocrite, first take the plank out of your own eye, and then you will see clearly to remove the speck from your brother's eye" (Matthew 7:4-5).

So whenever you read the Bible, don't ask first what it says to someone else. First ask Jesus what he is saying to you in the Scripture. If you're a husband, make sure you're obeying what the Bible says to husbands before you start quoting the Bible to your wife. If you're a wife, listen to God's instructions for wives before you start correcting your husband. If you're rich, make sure you hear the Bible's warnings to rich people, not its warnings to the lazy. If you're poor or in trouble, make sure you haven't brought it on yourself before you start blaming it on bias and oppression by others. Apply the Bible to yourself personally before you apply it to anyone else.

The fifth principle to guide your use of the Bible is this: *Always use Scripture with love*. This takes us right back to the fact that Jesus is the focus of Scripture, and that ultimate truth is not just a thing but a Person. Because truth is personal, and because it is grounded in Jesus—in the God who is love—we need love to hear what God is saying, and we need love to communicate God's truth to others. We need a heart that loves God in order to hear what he tells us without resenting it, and we need a heart that loves others in order to speak God's truth to them in a way that builds them up and doesn't tear them down.

Those are five basic principles for using the Bible properly instead of brandishing it like a drunkard with a thornbush. First, get right with God. Second, listen to the whole Bible as a unity. Third, focus on Jesus. Fourth, apply Scripture to yourself personally, not just to others. And fifth, always use Scripture with love. These aren't five separate things. They go together. To the degree that you use the Bible this way, God is bringing you closer to him and to his truth. You experience blessing in your own life, and you become a blessing to others.

If, however, your heart isn't right with God, if you're picking and choosing Bible verses that suit you, if Christ is not filling your heart and directing your mind, if you're using the Bible as a weapon against others instead of letting it rebuke and correct you, if you're not motivated by love for God and others, then you and your Bible become a curse rather than a blessing. The only way to reverse this is to realize what you've been doing and to repent and turn back to God. Stop acting like a drunkard waving roses. Stop your sinning. Stop your excuses. Stop misusing God's precious truth. Stop defiling his holy name. Ask God to forgive you for Jesus' sake and make you a new person.

Dealing With Wounds

What if you have been wounded by someone else's misuse of the Bible? Maybe they quoted some part of the Bible and twisted its meaning to justify their wrongdoing. Or maybe they simply claimed to be Bible-believing Christians but did rotten things anyway. We can pray that God will change such people—and he does change many—but there will always be some hypocrites around, and even people who are true Christians will sometimes use the Bible wrongly. The question is, How are you going to deal with it if you're the one who's been hurt?

It's terrible when such things happen, but don't double the tragedy by letting someone else's foolishness make a fool of you. Don't let the wounds inflicted by someone else keep you from God's Word in the Bible. Remember, God hates the misuse of the Bible even more than you do. Why else would he say, "Like a thornbush in a drunkard's hand is a proverb in the mouth of a fool"? Don't let a fool's misuse of the truth turn you against the truth. Otherwise, you become a fool yourself. Instead, believe in God. Believe that even if people misuse God's Word, his Word is true. Leave behind the memories of hypocrites who abused the Bible, and learn to enjoy the truth that God himself gives you.

Chapter 17

Why Church?

Is it possible to steer clear of church and be a healthy Christian? Many people would say yes to that question. They believe in God; they pray; they consider themselves to be Christians; and they see little need for church.

Is it possible to steer clear of church and be a healthy Christian? Not if God knows what he's talking about. God's Book, the Bible, shows again and again that when people belong to Jesus, they also belong to his church. They attend public worship faithfully and are deeply involved in the life of the church. So if you think you can be a healthy Christian without the church, you're saying that you know better than God—not a good idea.

Why Stay Away?

I've come across many different reasons that people stay away from church. You might feel you have no other choice. You feel you have to work Sundays. If you don't, you fear that you could lose your job. Going to church and praising God may be fine, but going to work and pleasing your boss is what pays the bills. God will understand, won't he?

Or you want to get some extra sleep on Sunday mornings. Or you want to cut the grass and wash the car. Or you want to go shopping. Or you plan your weekend around a trip to the beach or a round of golf or a sports event. Taking time out to go to church could mess up your weekend plans.

Then again, you might stay away from church because a member of the church or one of its leaders did something that turned you off. You figure, "If that's what the church is like, who needs it?" You want nothing to do with your old church, and you're not eager to find another one, either. Why hang around with a bunch of hypocrites?

Maybe you stay away from church because you feel just plain uncomfortable there. If you try going to church some Sunday, you feel out of place. Everybody but you seems to know when to stand up and when to sit down. Everybody there seems to know each other, but you don't know a soul, and hardly anyone talks with you or makes you feel welcome. Why go back to a situation that makes you feel so awkward?

Or maybe you have a very different reason for feeling awkward and staying away from church. You've belonged to a church for years. You know most of the people, and they know you. Then you go through marriage problems and divorce, or you go through something else that makes you feel guilty and embarrassed. You can't bear to face all those people. You'd rather steer clear of the church.

Those are a few reasons why people say they stay away from church. But in a way, these are beside the point. No matter what your reason for staying away, the first question to deal with is: Are there any good reasons for going? Many people stay home from church, not because they have any particular reason for staying away, but because they lack a reason for going. If nothing important happens in church, then almost any activity is better than wasting your time there. On the other hand, if the reasons in favor of church are strong enough, then you really have no choice but to get involved, no matter what your reasons have been for staying away.

God Says So

If you think faith is purely private, a "me and Jesus" thing, you're fooling yourself. You might ask, "Who says you need church?" God says so. Just look at some of the ways that God describes the church in the Bible.

The Bible calls the church *God's household*, God's family. The church is home for all who belong to God. So if you stay away from the church, you're either running away from home or you're not part of God's family at all.

The Bible speaks of the church as *the bride of Christ*. The Lord sees in her a beauty that becomes more and more radiant. He shares with her a deep love and intimacy. The church is more precious to Christ than a bride to her husband. If you don't love the church, your attitude is at odds with Jesus.

The Bible also calls the church *the body of Christ*. Each Christian is a part of that body. Obviously, for any body part to be alive and active, it must be connected to the body, so each Christian must be connected to the church. As the body of Christ, the church is alive with the Spirit of Christ and carries on the work of Jesus in the world. God himself calls us to be part of his church, not only to see the beauty of Jesus, who embodies God in human flesh, but also to see and take part in the beauty of the church, where flesh and blood people live in the power of the Holy Spirit.

Why church? Because it's the family of God, the bride of Christ, the body of Christ. Even at its ugliest, even when it is least attractive, any genuine church has in it a beauty and a power you can't find apart from the church. Why church? Because God says so. Why church? Because you and I need it.

The Bible makes it clear that when people put their faith in Jesus and are filled with the Holy Spirit, they don't just go their separate ways to do their own thing. No, they become part of the church through baptism. Baptism is the sign and seal of being washed in Jesus' blood and being raised again to new life. Baptism also marks people as new members of the church. Through baptism, they are added to the community of believers.

In the time shortly after Jesus' resurrection and the outpouring of the Holy Spirit, newly baptized people "devoted themselves to the apostles' teaching and to the fellowship, to the breaking of bread and to prayer" (Acts 2:42). In just one sentence, we have a four-fold answer to the question, "Why church?" First, for teaching. Second, for fellowship. Third, for breaking bread. Fourth, for prayer.

The Apostle's Teaching

Why church? First, because church is where we can devote
ourselves to the apostles' teaching. In the time of the New Testament church, the apostles were present in person to teach the
new believers. Today, the apostles have died and gone to heaven,
but they still teach us through their God-inspired writings in the
Bible.

The apostles teach us about Jesus—who he is, what he did,
and what he taught. They teach us the great plans and purposes
of God as they have unfolded in the history of salvation. They
teach us what it means to follow Christ in our own life and situation. Every church that is truly Christian rings with the teaching
of the apostles. Every church that is truly Christian stands on the
Bible. A church cannot stand on a few pleasant ideas or scholarly
suggestions. The church's foundation is the apostles' teaching,
which comes from Christ and reveals Christ.

We are "members of God's household, built on the foundation of the apostles and prophets, with Christ Jesus himself as
the chief cornerstone" (Ephesians 2:19-20). To build our lives on
truth, we need "the church of the living God, the pillar and
foundation of the truth" (1 Timothy 3:15).

You may be thinking, "Okay, so maybe I do need the apostles' teaching. But why church? Why not just read the Bible on
my own, or listen to Bible-based programs on radio and TV?"
I'm certainly in favor of Bible reading, and for sixteen years I was
an international gospel broadcaster, so I'm not against media
ministry. But to get the full benefit of the apostles' teaching,
don't just listen to broadcasts. Be involved in a congregation in
your community. There is something about being together with
God's people in a place of worship that brings a special sense of
God's presence. The people praise God together, and together
they confess their need for God to forgive their sins. The preacher speaks with special authority, and the people listen with special openness. In a local church, the minister applies the Bible's
teaching to the needs of a particular community and congregation in a way that a media ministry can't.

What's more, when you have questions about God's Word, or personal problems that you're wrestling with, your pastor or another fellow Christian can talk with you face-to-face about those needs. You have opportunities in a local congregation for Bible discussion groups and for personal conversations about how the apostles' teaching should affect your life. You can't get this just studying on your own or listening to media preachers. You need to be an active part of your local church.

Fellowship

Now let's consider the second vital aspect of the church: the fellowship. Church is the special community where we share in the fellowship of believers.

I remember talking with a man who stopped going to church because he was upset with his local congregation. He stayed home Sundays and watched a preacher on TV. When I urged him not to cut himself off from his church, he said, "I get what I need by watching the TV minister."

Later, we spoke together again. His son had been killed in a tragic accident. The grieving father found that there are some things you don't get by watching TV. The TV preacher wasn't there in the man's home to embrace him and pray with him and speak words of hope and comfort. The TV screen doesn't weep with those who weep. The only ones who could give this man the support he needed were the pastor and people of his church.

During my years as a broadcaster, I heard from a lot of people facing difficulties. Many of them had no church. My staff and I tried to help them at a distance. But there were limits to what we could do. We couldn't replace the fellowship of a local church. So we constantly encouraged people to find a church. When you're facing illness, or the loss of a loved one, or financial problems, or a family crisis, you don't just need good advice over the airwaves. You need people who are right there, Christian brothers and sisters who can support you in tough times.

I know that the church has its faults, that the fellowship is often far from perfect. After all, the church is a fellowship of sinners who still have plenty of changing to do. The people don't always get along very well. But I also know that when the going gets tough, the people pull together to support the one who is hurting. Time and again I've heard people facing a crisis tell me, "Now I really know what the communion of the saints is. I don't know how I would have made it without the prayers and support of the people in my church."

The church's fellowship does more than just get us through times of crisis. Christians devote themselves to fellowship because in the church the whole is greater than the parts. Like a body, the church has many parts, each with its own purpose.

You might think that the things you're good at aren't as important to the church as the things other people are good at. But that's no way to look at it. Wouldn't it be crazy if a foot said, "Because I am not a hand, I do not belong to the body" or if the ear said, "Because I am not an eye, I do not belong to the body?" What if the body were one big eyeball? It would be grotesque—and how would it hear? What if it were one big ear? How would it smell? It's a good thing God gave the body many different parts and arranged them the way he wanted.

The same applies to the church. God brings together many unique individuals, who are gifted in many different ways. If you're a Christian but you think the church can do just fine without you, think again. Every part is important.

The church needs you, and you need the church. "The eye cannot say to the hand, 'I don't need you!' And the head cannot say to the feet, 'I don't need you!'" (1 Corinthians 12:21) It would be insane for one part to say to the rest of the body, "I don't need you." What happens when a part is amputated from the body? It dies and decays. If you say to the body of Christ, "I don't need you. I can do just fine on my own," your soul will decay. To live and grow, you need to be part of the body.

You need the church, and the church needs you. Every part needs the others. If one part suffers, they all suffer. If one part flourishes, the others benefit. That's how God designed our physical bodies, and that's how he designed the body of Christ.

It's not just "me and Jesus." It's "we and Jesus." When Christians devote themselves to the fellowship, they all benefit from each other's God-given abilities, and they accomplish many things together that they couldn't do alone.

We also need the fellowship so we can be accountable to each other. The world is full of negative peer pressure, but the church can provide positive peer pressure. As the Bible says, "Let us consider how we may spur one another on toward love and good deeds. Let us not give up meeting together, as some are in the habit of doing, but let us encourage one another" (Hebrews 10:24-25). When we get tired and discouraged in trying to follow Christ, we need a boost from others. When we fall into sin and bad habits, we need to be confronted by others. This involves more than just showing up for Sunday services, of course. It means really getting to know each other, often in the setting of small groups or close friendships. It means placing ourselves under the authority of the church, not just doing our own thing.

The church is a setting for loving fellowship, where we can start loving others as Christ has loved us. Jesus says, "A new command I give you: Love one another. As I have loved you, so you must love one another. By this all men will know that you are my disciples, if you love one another" (John 13:34-35).

Breaking Bread

Why church? So far we've seen our need for the apostles' teaching and the loving fellowship of God's people. Now let's look at a third reason: the breaking of bread. In church God's people gather around the table of the Lord. As we eat bread broken from a loaf, we participate in the body of the Lord Jesus, sacrificed for our salvation. As we drink wine, we drink in the blood of Christ, poured out to give us life.

A living faith isn't just a matter of thinking about Jesus. A living faith feasts on Jesus, again and again and again. Jesus said, "Whoever eats my flesh and drinks my blood has eternal life, and I will raise him up at the last day. For my flesh is real food, and my blood is real drink. Whoever eats my flesh and drinks my blood remains in me and I in him" (John 6:54-56). The Lord's Supper isn't just a visual aid or a meaningless ritual. It's a spiritual feast, and we can't afford to miss it.

Why church? Because it is in church, gathered around the Lord's Table, that we find Jesus coming to us and giving us his body and blood to nourish our souls for eternal life. He doesn't come physically, but he does come really, by his Holy Spirit. As our mouths take in bread and wine, our souls take in the living Christ and the benefits of his body and blood given for us.

Prayer

A fourth reason for church is prayer. The Christians in the New Testament church got together to pray. You might wonder, "Why go to church to pray? I can pray by myself just fine." It's true that personal prayer is important and that you can pray any time, anywhere. But praying together with others is also important. When God's people come together, whether as a large congregation or in a small prayer meeting, their prayers take on added power. Jesus said, "I tell you that if two of you on earth agree about anything you ask for, it will be done for you by my Father in heaven. For where two or three come together in my name, there am I with them" (Matthew 18:19-20). Why church? Because there God's people pray together with one heart and praise God together with one voice.

Listen again to Acts 2:42. "They devoted themselves to the apostles' teaching and to the fellowship, to the breaking of bread and to prayer." That's what the first Christians did together as a church, and that's a good summary of why you and I need to involve ourselves in the church still today.

Acts 2 goes on to tell about the dynamic life in that church. There were miracles. Christians were selling their goods to share with fellow believers who didn't have enough. Every day they were praising God in the temple and enjoying each other's company in their homes. And the Lord kept adding to their number those who were being saved. Still today, whatever its faults may be, a truly Christian congregation is a setting where God's power is at work in amazing ways, where God's people give of themselves to help others, and where they bring joy to each other's hearts and to God. Why church? Because it's dynamic. It's where prayers are answered, where amazing things happen.

The Perfect Church?

Are you looking for a perfect church? I'm not. If I could find a perfect church, I couldn't join it, or it would no longer be perfect. I need a church that has room for a sinner like me. And you need a church that has room for a sinner like you.

Besides, there is no perfect church this side of heaven. If you think you've discovered one, you don't know the people well enough. No matter how great a church might be, it is made up of people who struggle with sin. No matter what church you go to, there will be some hypocrites who aren't Christians at all, and even the genuine Christians will still be a long way from perfect.

Unfortunately, some people can't handle being part of an imperfect church. The moment they find an imperfection, they either boycott church altogether or resort to church hopping.

If you're a boycotter, you use the church's flaws as an excuse to stay away. Your boycott may take the form of ignoring religion completely, or it may take the form of trying to get your spiritual nourishment on your own without being part of any group. You depend on books or broadcasts to help you enjoy a "me and Jesus" relationship, but you stay away from church so that you can avoid the frustrations of dealing with real, flesh-and-blood people with all their weaknesses and failings.

If you're a church hopper, on the other hand, you don't feel right not going to church at all. You go to church, but you're never in the same place for long. The moment you find something you don't like, you're off to look for a better church. You hop from one church to another to another, always hoping to find a congregation that suits you perfectly. But you never do.

If you're a church hopper or a boycotter, it's time you realized that you won't find a perfect church. You need to find a church, commit yourself to it, and then stick with it.

When you read about the New Testament church, you might be tempted to say, "Oh, I'd love to go to a church like that, but churches today don't have what it takes." But don't kid yourself. If you read the Bible, you find that the church back then struggled with its own problems and scandals. And if you look honestly at the church today, you find it's not as bad as you'd like to think when you're looking for excuses not to be involved. There are some churches so corrupt and so unbiblical that you're better off staying away, but that doesn't mean you can't find an authentic church. Be glad the church isn't too good for you, and don't act like you're too good to join the saved sinners who are in the church.

Don't pretend you've got better things to do. What is more important than devoting yourself to the apostles' teaching and to the fellowship, to the breaking of bread and to prayer? Find a Bible-believing, Christ-honoring church, and stick with it. You'll be amazed what happens.

Chapter 18

Knowing By Faith

What is faith? A feeling? A guess? Is faith whatever opinion you happen to have about spiritual things? Is faith a blind leap where you have no idea what the facts are? Is faith a wager where you bet on Jesus just in case he's for real? Is faith a fantasy that makes you happier but has no basis in reality? Is faith a wish, wanting something so much that it comes true? Is faith visualization, making something more likely to happen by picturing it in your mind? Is faith a decision, a commitment? Is faith a value, something you hold dear? Is faith a tradition? People sometimes speak of their "faith tradition."

Some of these ideas aren't entirely wrong, but notice what they all have in common: none involves knowing. There's a saying, "If you knew, you wouldn't need faith." Is faith the opposite of knowledge? Many people think so. But they are mistaken.

Real faith is knowledge of reality! Hebrews 11:1 says, "Now faith is the reality of what is hoped for, the proof of what is not seen" (HCSB). Another translation says, "Faith makes us sure of what we hope for and gives us proof of what we cannot see" (CEV). Faith deals with reality that is unseen but substantial; faith involves solid, accurate knowledge.

Sure Knowledge

What is true faith? Here's how the Heidelberg Catechism answers that question:

True faith is not only a *sure knowledge* by which I hold as true all that God has revealed to us in Scripture; it is also a *wholehearted trust*, which the Holy Spirit creates in me

by the gospel, that God has freely granted, not only to
others but to me also, forgiveness of sins, eternal righteousness and salvation. These are gifts of sheer grace,
granted solely by Christ's merit (Q&A 21).

Faith involves the vital element of personal, wholehearted trust
that the Holy Spirit creates in us. It also includes sure knowledge
of truths that God reveals. Faith involves knowing. In speaking
of faith as sure knowledge, the Catechism is echoing the Bible.
Here's a sample of biblical statements that speak of knowing by
faith.

"You will *understand* the fear of the Lord and find the
knowledge of God. For the Lord gives *wisdom*, and from his
mouth come *knowledge* and *understanding*" (Proverbs 2:5-6).
This passage does not speak of guesswork or educated opinions;
it speaks of knowledge.

Jesus tells his followers, "To you it has been given to *know*
the secrets of the kingdom of heaven, but to them it has not been
given" (Matthew 13:11). People who believe in Jesus have God-
given knowledge, Christ-given knowledge.

"No one has ever seen God; the only God, who is at the Father's side, has made him *known*" (John 1:18). Jesus, God the
Son, came from the Father's side to make him known. This
comes through clearly in a prayer that Jesus prayed to his Father
the night before he went to the cross.

"This is eternal life: that they may *know* you, the only
true God, and Jesus Christ, whom you have sent... O
righteous Father, even though the world does not know
you, I *know* you, and these *know* that you have sent me. I
have made *known* to them your name, and I will continue
to make it *known*, that the love with which you have
loved me may be in them, and I in them" (John 17:3, 25-
26 ESV).

Like Jesus, his apostles speak of faith as knowledge. The
apostle Peter writes:

May grace and peace be multiplied to you in the
knowledge of God and of Jesus our Lord. His divine pow-

er has granted to us all things that pertain to life and godliness, through the *knowledge* of him who called us to his
own glory and excellence... But grow in the grace and
knowledge of our Lord and Savior Jesus Christ (2 Peter
1:2-3, 3:18).

The apostle Paul similarly links faith and knowledge. He
speaks of "the *faith* of God's elect and the *knowledge of the truth*
that leads to godliness—a *faith* and *knowledge* resting on the
hope of eternal life, which *God, who does not lie,* promised before
the beginning of time" (Titus 1:1). Shortly before Paul was killed
for his faith in Christ, he wrote, "I *know* whom I have *believed*"
(2Tim 1:12). Paul doesn't guess or wish or imagine; he knows!

The apostle John repeatedly speaks of believing in Jesus as
knowledge.

I write these things to you who believe in the name of the
Son of God so that you may *know* that you have eternal
life... We *know* that anyone born of God does not continue to sin... We *know* that we are children of God and
that the whole world is under the control of the evil one.
We *know* also that the Son of God has come and has giv-
en us *understanding*, so that we may *know* him who is
true. And we are in him who is *true*—even in his Son Jesus Christ. He is the *true* God and eternal life (I John
5:13, 18-21).

Notice John's words: "know... know... know... know...
know... true... true... true."

According to Jesus and all the biblical writers, faith in Jesus
isn't just feeling or opinion; faith is knowledge of reality.

Faith and Other Ways of Knowing

Faith is knowing. In fact, faith has much in common with
other ways of knowing.

One way we know things is by accepting them as *givens*
without needing any proof. We just know them. We take them
as a starting point and standard for evaluating other things we
believe. We know as givens some things that are not specifically

Christian; likewise, we know some Christian truths as givens that don't require further proof.

Another way that we come to know things is *testimony*. Much of what we know about life and the world comes through accepting testimony, believing what we're told, learning from others, receiving their knowledge and embracing it for ourselves. Likewise, much of what we know about God comes from accepting the testimony of others.

A third way of knowing is through our *faculties*. We have abilities that give us knowledge of things around us and within us. We have sense faculties such as seeing, hearing, tasting, smelling and touching. We have mental faculties such as memory and logic. When these faculties are working properly in the right kind of setting, they give us knowledge. Faith, too, involves a faculty that gives us knowledge when working properly in the right setting.

A fourth way of knowing is through *relating*. We know other people through personal interaction, through our dealings with them and their dealings with us, by conversation and communication. So it is with God. Knowing God involves relating by personal interaction.

Let's look at each of these four ways of knowing in more depth and detail. We'll see how faith overlaps them and sometimes surpasses them.

Givens: Starting Point and Standard

All knowledge starts with accepting some things as givens. These presuppositions, these first principles or assumptions, require no proof. They are basic for knowing other things, and they are a standard for evaluating other ideas. Givens, or first principles, include: the world is real; my senses are experiencing real things; my mind can know truths; other persons are real and not just illusions; memories really happened; some things are right, and others are wrong.

We accept givens without proof. Has anyone proved to you that the world is real and that your senses are experiencing real things? Has anyone proved to you that you're not just dreaming everything? No, you don't wait for proofs that the world is real and that your senses are in touch with real things; you just assume these things—and you are right.

Has anyone proved to you that your mind can know truths? No, you assume this. Before you can know anything at all, you must assume that you have a mind capable of knowing things.

Has anyone proved to you that other people are real and not just illusions in your mind? No, but you know they are real without needing proof. You don't need evidence and arguments before you can know they are real; you take it as a given that the people you meet really do exist outside your mind.

Has anyone proved to you that your memories really happened? Has anyone proved to you that your memories weren't all implanted in your brain five minutes ago, filling your mind with a lifetime's worth of things that didn't happen? You don't have proof that your memory connects with a real past; you assume it. You take it as a given, and you are right to do so.

Has anyone proved to you that kindness is good and cruelty is evil, that faithfulness is good and betrayal is evil? No, but you know deep down that there's a difference between right and wrong. It's a given and doesn't need to be proven.

Some of our most important knowledge must be accepted as givens without proof. Knowing has to start somewhere; it can't all be proven on the basis of prior knowledge. Whatever we call these givens—presuppositions, assumptions, first principles— they are knowledge. The fact that there is no way of proving them does not make them irrational. These givens form a starting point and standard for everything else we know.

Not every starting point, not everything that somebody takes as a given, is correct. For example, atheistic science has a starting point. Richard Lewontin, a geneticist at Harvard, says,

> We take the side of [atheistic] science in spite of the patent absurdity of some of its constructs ... because we have a prior commitment, a commitment to materialism. It is not that the methods and institutions of science

somehow compel us to accept a material explanation...
but, on the contrary, that we are forced by our a priori
adherence to material causes ... no matter how counterin-
tuitive. Moreover, that materialism is absolute, for we
cannot allow a Divine Foot in the door.

Lewinton assumes as a first principle that God is not real, that
nothing exists except matter, that everything has a material explanation. He accepts this without proof, no matter how absurd
it sometimes seems, no matter how it goes against our sense of
things, no matter how much evidence seems to indicate the reality of God. He assumes as an absolute first principle that no belief
in God can be allowed into his mind: "We cannot allow a Divine
foot in the door." For Lewinton and other materialists, that is a
given—or, dare I say it, an article of faith.

A first principle may be hard or impossible to prove or disprove, but you can at least ask whether it fits with your other
first principles or contradicts them. If you assume that matter is
all that exists, how well does that fit with the assumption that
your mind has the ability to know things outside it, and the assumption that the world is real and has features that are knowable? If your materialism means your brain is a randomly evolved
blob of meat, can you still assume that your mind has the ability
to know things outside it? If the universe is only matter flying
randomly through space, should you expect to find any real patterns within it that the mind can make sense of? If you assume
there is no Mind who created the universe, that assumption
clashes with the assumptions that your mind has the ability to
know and that the world is knowable. Lewinton's first principle
of atheistic materialism contradicts first principles that are essential for any knowing. Thought itself is an act of faith that the
mind can know something.

It is idle to talk always of the alternative of reason and
faith. It is an act of faith to assert that our thoughts have
any relation to reality at all. If you are merely a skeptic,
you must sooner or later ask yourself the question, "Why
should *anything* go right; even observation and deduction?

Why should not good logic be as misleading as bad logic?" They are both movements in the brain of a bewil-
dered ape (G. K. Chesterton).

Beware of accepting a first principle that destroys other first
principles. That's what atheistic materialism does.

On the other hand, faith in the Creator is a first principle
that supports other first principles. If we begin with God, we
don't destroy understanding; we gain understanding. The church
father Augustine said, "I believe in order that I may understand."
Anselm, who lived about a thousand years after Jesus' resurrection, spoke of "faith seeking understanding." The Bible itself
says, "By faith we understand that the universe was created by
the word of God, so that what is seen was not made out of things
that are visible" (Hebrews 11:2). By faith we understand! Faith
does not destroy thought. Faith brings understanding.

By faith we understand that we have minds that can know
and a world that can be known. Faith recognizes Jesus as the one
who made the entire world by his wisdom and the one who gives
wisdom to the human mind. "In the beginning was the Word
[*Logos*], and the Word was with God, and the Word was God...
The true light that gives light to every man was coming into the
world" (John 1:1-14). Jesus is the eternal Word, the *Logos*, the
logic of the world and the light of human intellect.

Faith doesn't have to prove God; belief in God can be a first
principle, a starting point. This is not inventing a God who isn't
there; it is beginning with the God who is there.

Imagination projects unreal images out of the mind and
seeks to attach reality to them. Faith creates nothing; it
simply reckons upon that which is already there. God and
the spiritual world are real. We can reckon upon them
with as much assurance as we reckon upon the familiar
world around us. Spiritual things are there (or rather we
should say here) inviting our attention and challenging
our trust (A. W. Tozer).

It is rational to presuppose some things as givens without any
proof. Thinking has to start somewhere. We can't avoid first

principles; we just need sound first principles. Starting with right presuppositions gives us a firm foundation for other knowledge and a measuring stick to evaluate various claims. Given that God created the universe and that God created our minds, we have a first principle that fits with and supports other first principles, such as the assumption that our minds have the ability to know and that the world is real and has patterns that can be known.

Knowing by faith overlaps other ways of knowing. This is certainly true of presuppositions. All of us, whether religious or not, accept some beliefs as givens, as presuppositions that need no proof. Similarly, key truths of Christianity can be accepted as givens, as true knowledge not requiring proof. God's revelation in his written Word, the Bible, and in his living Word, Jesus, can be accepted by faith as givens, as first principles to ground our worldview and to provide a standard for deciding what else is true. You don't need to prove that God's revelation is true. You can take it as a starting point. What could be a better starting point? What is more certain than God's own truth? Faith can accept as givens the reality of God, of his creative work, and of Jesus as the one who has established the patterns and logic of all reality. Believing these givens is not mere opinion; it is firm knowledge of solid truth.

Testimony

Testimony is another area in which knowing by faith overlaps other ways of knowing. Much of what we know comes through accepting testimony, believing what we're told. In our early years, we learn a lot from parents and family members. As we grow up, our knowledge of math, science, and history comes mostly from accepting what we're told by teachers and books. Our knowledge of parenting, gardening, cooking, business, and much else comes mostly from accepting what we're told.

Some skeptics have insisted, "It's irrational to believe something just because someone else told you. You need to discover it and prove it for yourself." But it would be irrational to disbelieve all testimony. Rejecting everything you're told would make you an ignoramus. Very little of what you know about math, science, business, or parenting comes through your own personal discoveries and experiments. If you insisted on not believing anything except what you discovered by personal observation, you could only have a tiny fraction of the knowledge that's available to you. Believing the testimony of reliable people is a very important way of knowing. Even in court cases, our knowledge often comes from testimony. If we dismissed testimony in courts and elsewhere in life, we wouldn't know very much. We need to accept testimony.

If it's okay to learn about many areas of life from the testimony of reliable people, why would it not be okay to learn about God and his ways by accepting testimony, by trusting what others tell us? Many of us came to know who God is and how he relates to us by learning from trustworthy parents or from friends. They told us many things we didn't know, and through their testimony we came to know those things for ourselves.

Besides the testimony of Christian people, there's another level of testimony that is far greater. The Bible gives human authors' eyewitness testimony to God and his actions in Christ. When the people of Israel received the Ten Commandments at Mount Sinai, they saw fire and heard the thunder of God's voice. They were eyewitnesses of Moses coming down from the mountain with the Ten Commandments written in stone. The Bible records eyewitness testimony of this and many other things God has said and done. Jesus' dear friend, the apostle John, wrote,

> That which was from the beginning, which we have heard, which we have seen with our eyes, which we have looked at and our hands have touched—this we proclaim concerning the Word of life... We proclaim to you what we have seen and heard" (1 John 1:1-3).

Likewise, the apostle Peter emphasized that the apostles were not making stuff up but wrote as eyewitnesses: "We did not follow cleverly invented stories when we told you about the power and coming of our Lord Jesus Christ, but we were eyewitnesses of his majesty" (2 Peter 1:16).

The Bible deserves to be believed, not only because it provides eyewitness testimony to God's words and actions culminating in Jesus Christ, but also because the Holy Spirit guided these eyewitnesses. The Spirit gave them accurate memory of what they saw and heard, and the Spirit guided them to write in the Bible exactly what God wanted them to write.

As the Holy Spirit guided Bible writers, he guides Bible readers. As the Holy Spirit testifies through words on a page, he also testifies through working in a heart. There is a double movement. When the outer testimony of Scripture produces belief in the Son of God, we have the inner testimony of God's Spirit. Faith accepts God's testimony. The Bible puts it this way:

> We accept man's testimony, but God's testimony is greater because it is the testimony of God, which he has given about his Son. Anyone who believes in the Son of God has this testimony in his heart. Anyone who does not believe God has made him out to be a liar, because he has not believed the testimony God has given about his Son. And this is the testimony: God has given us eternal life, and this life is in his Son. He who has the Son has life; he who does not have the Son of God does not have life. I write these things to you who believe in the name of the Son of God so that you may know that you have eternal life (1 John 5:9-13).

By faith in God's testimony, you know God's reality, and you know that you have eternal life. The testimony of God does not produce mere opinion or feeling. You know!

Accepting testimony is a major way we know all sorts of things about the world; likewise, accepting testimony is a major way to know God. Knowing by faith involves accepting the testimony of people who know God, accepting the testimony of God's Word in the Bible, and accepting the testimony of God's Spirit as he seals the Bible's message on your heart. If we gain valuable knowledge by believing the testimony of ordinary humans, then surely we can gain valuable knowledge by believing what God himself says.

Faculties Working Properly

A third aspect of knowing is knowledge gained through our senses and other abilities. We have knowledge when our faculties are working properly in a suitable setting for which those faculties were designed to produce true beliefs.

For example, take the faculty of seeing. Suppose you're looking at a chair. You're able to see it because the chair is really there, light is bouncing off the chair, and that light is entering your eyes. Your eyes and brain are working properly to produce knowledge of the chair. But suppose instead that there is no light in the room. Then you can't see the chair because it's not a proper setting for seeing: no light is reflected from the chair to your eyes. Or imagine yet another scenario. You're in a room, the light is there, and the chair is there, but you are high on drugs. You don't see a chair; you see a pink elephant. Obviously, it's not enough to have a faculty for seeing. To produce real knowledge, your faculty must be operating in the right setting, and your faculty must be working properly.

Although it's possible for the setting to be wrong or for a faculty to malfunction, there are many times when a faculty is in the right setting and is working properly. Then we gain knowledge. Our faculties give us access to many kinds of knowledge. We have sense faculties such as seeing, hearing, tasting, smelling and touching. We have mental faculties like memory and logic. When these faculties are working properly in the right kind of surroundings, they give us knowledge.

This is true of knowing in general, and it is true of knowing by faith. You might think that faith is totally different from knowledge gained through the senses and other faculties. But what if we have a faculty for sensing God? What if faith is what happens when our God-sense (our faculty designed to produce knowledge of God) is made healthy and is in a setting where God is showing something of himself for us to know? In that case, faith is knowledge!

The physical senses involve organs receiving signals. You see only if you have eyes that work and light from an object reaches you. You hear only if you have ears that work and something sends sound waves. You taste only if your taste buds work and something is in your mouth. You smell only if your nose is working and molecules from something are in the air. You feel touch only if your skin and nerves are working and something touches you. That's how our bodily senses work: by organs receiving signals from something outside us.

Something similar occurs with our God-sense. The Bible uses sensory language about receiving signals from God.

- *Taste* and *see* that the Lord is good (Psalm 34:8).
- My sheep *hear* my voice (John 10:27).
- How sweet are your words to my *taste*, sweeter than honey to my mouth! (Psalm 119:103).
- For we are to God the *aroma* of Christ among those who are being saved and those who are perishing. To the one we are the smell of death; to the other, the *fragrance* of life (2 Corinthians 2:15-16).
- Were not our hearts *burning* within us while he talked with us on the road and opened the Scriptures to us? (Luke 24:32).

Tasting, seeing, hearing, smelling an aroma, feeling a burning within—something happens within us as God comes near and shares himself with us.

Spiritual faculties sense and know things by experience, not just by description. Although you sometimes can gain valuable knowledge from descriptions of things, there are other kinds of knowledge that you can't get except by experiencing them through your senses. You know red by seeing it. If you're blind or colorblind, no description of red is going to help you know what red is. You know music by hearing it. You could look at musical notes on a page, or you could have someone talk to you about music theory, and this might give you knowledge of sorts. But if you never heard music, there would be much that you couldn't know about it. You know a scent by smelling it. You know honey by tasting it. Experience gives you a kind of knowledge that description alone cannot give.

So it is with knowledge of God. You know things of God by seeing with your inner eye. You know the music of God's voice by hearing with your inner ear. You know the scent of the gospel when it smells good to your inner self. You know the taste of God's truth not just when you mumble, "I believe the Bible is true," but when your God-sense is feasting on the delicious bread of life. You know God's burning reality not just through doctrinal description but by feeling his flame within. When your heart burns within you, when the flame of the Holy Spirit warms your God-sense, then you're experiencing something of God's reality.

These experiences are not just weird things in the imagination that have no contact with reality. These experiences occur when our heart-organs, our inner spiritual faculties, work properly, receive signals from God, and gain knowledge of God through inner experience. Inner experience can bring you real knowledge of the real God, even if some people don't have such experiences and don't believe God is real. Just because other people don't see something doesn't mean you don't know what you're seeing. Sometimes we think of knowledge as something that everybody ought to be able to know and prove to others. But it's possible for one person to see the Grand Canyon and know its splendors, while others don't see it because they are blind or because they are located a thousand miles from the Grand Canyon. There are some kinds of knowledge that simply aren't experienced or known by everybody. By faith Christians see divine reality, even if others don't see it. Our sight is knowledge, even if unbelievers lack a renewed eye or lack God's light. The Bible says, "We know that we are children of God, and that the whole world is under the control of the evil one" (1 John 5:19). There is much that people cannot know as long as they are under the control of the evil one. "The god of this world [Satan] has blinded the minds of the unbelievers, to keep them from seeing the light of the gospel of the glory of Christ, who is the image of God" (2 Corinthians 4:4). Just because not everybody agrees with you doesn't mean you don't know what you know by faith.

Faith sees and knows. "For God who said, 'Let light shine out of darkness' made his light shine in our hearts to give us the light of the knowledge of the glory of God in the face of Christ" (2 Corinthians 4:6). When God makes his light shine in your heart, your God-sense knows that God is real and glorious and that Christ is his revelation. Jesus says, "Blessed are the pure in heart, for they shall see God" (Matthew 5:8). Faith sees and faith knows. The apostle Paul writes,

> I keep asking that the God of our Lord Jesus Christ, the glorious Father, may give you the Spirit of wisdom and revelation, so that you may *know* him better. I pray also that the *eyes of your heart* may be enlightened in order that you may *know* the hope to which he has called you, the riches of his glorious inheritance in the saints, and his incomparably great power for us who believe. (Ephesians 1:17-19)

God has designed us with eyes in our heart, a way of sensing him. Everybody has a God-sense. We all have eyes in the heart. But having eyes doesn't help if those eyes aren't working properly. Some people may be blind. Others have partial cataracts and need those cataracts removed from their eyes so that they can see more clearly and fully. Those who have never known God need the eyes of their heart opened. Those of us who do know God and are already believers need our inner eyes opened even wider. We pray that God will make our inner eyes keener and that he will give more light to those eyes so that we can know him better than we already do.

By faith our heart-eyes see what mere eyeballs can't see. By faith, our heart-eyes see that God is real and that God is rewarding. "Whoever would draw near to God must believe that he exists and that he rewards those who seek him" (Hebrews 11:6). Moses was a man who saw God's reality and reward. "Moses considered the reproach of Christ greater wealth than the treasures of Egypt, for he was looking to the reward... he endured as seeing him who is invisible" (Hebrews 11:26-27). What a phrase! Seeing him who is invisible! You're not seeing him with your eyeballs because he's invisible, but you're seeing him with your heart-eyes. And what do you see? You see that it's better to suffer with Christ than to have the treasures of Egypt. You see that Christ on a cross is better than the world on a throne.

True knowledge comes when your faculties are working properly. Faith is the action of the reborn God-sense that takes in God's self-revelation. The Spirit creates faith by reviving the God-sense and speaking gospel truth in such a manner that you accept the facts, know those facts are meant for you personally, and delight in God and in the great things of the gospel. Sin blinds the God-sense or distorts it badly. But God renews the God-sense and communicates to it. God gives you a sense not only that he is real and glorious and good and loving and brings salvation, but that he does this for you. When your spiritual faculties are working properly and God is sending you his signals, then what you know by faith is real knowledge.

> Faith enables our spiritual sense to function. Where faith is defective the result will be inward insensibility and numbness toward spiritual things... Our trouble is that we have established bad thought habits. We habitually think of the visible world as real and doubt the reality of any other. Sin has so clouded the lenses of our hearts that we cannot see that other reality, the City of God, shining around us. The soul has eyes with which to see and ears with which to hear. Feeble they may be from long disuse, but by the life-giving touch of Christ they are now alive and capable of sharpest sight and most sensitive hearing. As we begin to focus upon God, the things of the spirit will take shape before our inner eyes. A new God-consciousness will seize upon us and we shall begin to taste and see and inwardly feel God, who is our life and our all (A. W. Tozer).

When our spiritual faculties are working properly, when our God-sense is healthy and God is shining his light into our hearts, then our faith knows God. This knowledge is as real as any knowledge gained through our physical senses.

Relating

In addition to givens, testimony, and faculties, there is a fourth area in which knowing by faith overlaps with how we know other things: relating. We know other persons by interaction. If I know a friend, I don't ask that friend, "Do you exist? Could you please prove your reality to me?" No, I interact with that friend, he interacts with me, and we communicate. So it is in relating to God. When God speaks to me and I speak to him in prayer, we are interacting. We know the personal God by interaction, by awareness of another Self making himself known to us and drawing us to know him.

Nearly everybody in the world has some sense of the reality of God. Conscience gives us a sense of right and wrong rooted in Someone who holds us to his standard. Sometimes when we're in the presence of fantastic created realities—stars, mountains, waterfalls, newborn babies—we have a sense of awe and gratitude come over us that goes beyond anything in the creation. We know that we're in the presence of Someone far greater than anything he's made. This is real knowledge. And our knowledge of God goes far beyond that. By faith we know what God has done for us in Jesus, paying for our sins, crediting to us Jesus' perfect life, and being our companion every day. We accept this by faith, and we go to God's throne in prayer.

When we relate to the Lord, he is not just a theory or a belief or an idea. God is personal. We're glad we know him, and we seek to know him better. This personal knowledge is the richest kind of knowledge. "We know that the Son of God has come and has given us understanding, so that we may know him who is true" (1 John 5:20). Jesus came into our world so that we would understand truth and especially so that we would know the real and living God by personal acquaintance. Jesus came to make him known.

The Holy Spirit brings God close to us and draws us close to him in a relationship of love.

This is how we know that he lives in us: We know it by the Spirit he gave us... We know that we live in him and

he in us, because he has given us of his Spirit. And we
have seen and testify that the Father has sent his Son to be
the Savior of the world. If anyone acknowledges that Jesus is the Son of God, God lives in him and he in God.
And so we know and rely on the love God has for us. God
is love. Whoever lives in love lives in God, and God in
him (1 John 3:24; 4:13-16).

Of all the ways of knowing by faith, this is the deepest and most
wonderful: interacting in love with the God who has loved us
from all eternity, and getting to know better the God who has
already begun to make himself known to us. It's reassuring to
know that God knows us totally, that there's nothing about us
that's going to surprise him, that he loves us in spite of the bad
things he knows, that he creates in us more and more of the
good things of Jesus, and that he moves us to love him in return.

Faith is Knowledge

Faith is not the opposite of knowledge; faith *is* knowledge.
When it comes to knowing things more generally, we count on
givens, testimony, faculties, and relating. Knowing by faith includes, combines, and surpasses these.

We accept some *givens* and take them as true, without question and without proof. It's rational to accept the reality of God
and things revealed by God as our starting point, as givens for
which we don't need proof.

We gain knowledge in many areas of life by *testimony*, by believing what reliable people tell us. When we accept the testimony of God's people and of God himself, our knowledge grows.
No testimony is more trustworthy than God's Word, the Bible.

We get knowledge through our *faculties*, our abilities working properly in an appropriate setting. Along with physical senses, the Lord has given us a God-sense, a heart faculty for sensing
God. Sin has clouded and distorted the God-sense, blinding the
eyes of the heart. But when God gives us new life, when we're
born again, the Holy Spirit restores that spiritual faculty, so that
we sense God's reality. We see His light. We taste His goodness.

We hear His voice. We breathe in his sweet aroma. We feel his touch and his fire within. Through the Spirit, our God-sense works better and better, and God shines more and more brightly, so that we come to know him more fully and clearly.

The highest form of knowing is *relating*. As we know other persons through personal interaction, so knowledge of God comes through personal interaction: loving and being loved, talking and listening.

Faith is knowledge that includes, combines, and surpasses these four elements of more ordinary knowing. By faith we take God's written Word, the Bible, and God's living Word, Jesus, as our starting point and standard for truth; we accept his testimony; we perceive his glory with our inner heart sense; and we embrace God's interaction with us.

Alvin Plantinga is a specialist in epistemology, the study of how we know what we know. He shows how knowing by faith is similar in some respects to other ways of knowing. At the same time, he shows how knowing by faith surpasses all other kinds of knowing. Dr. Plantinga writes,

> Faith is not to be *contrasted* with knowledge: faith *is* knowledge, knowledge of a certain special kind. It is special in at least two ways. First, [what is known] is of stunning significance, certainly the most important thing a person could possibly know. [Second] it is known by way of an extraordinary cognitive process or belief-producing mechanism. Christian belief is "revealed to our minds" by way of the Holy Spirit's inducing, in us, belief in the central message of Scripture.

Centuries before Alvin Plantinga, the reformer John Calvin wrote, "Faith is a firm and certain knowledge of God's benevolence towards us, founded upon the truth of the freely given promises in Christ, both revealed to our minds and sealed upon our hearts through the Holy Spirit." By faith we *know* God and where we stand with him. Faith is knowledge.

Chapter 19

Questions About Knowing By Faith

Christianity isn't just feeling; it is fact. Faith isn't mere opinion; it is knowledge. We *know* by faith. The instant we say this, questions arise.

- Is it arrogant to be confident in knowing God?
- Is it hateful intolerance to know Jesus is the way?
- Is it judgmental to say others are wrong?
- Can you really know you have eternal life?
- Is faith ever unclear or unsure?
- Why do we need faith if we have knowledge?
- Is it irrational to believe despite contrary evidence?

Let's look at each of these in more detail.

Is it arrogant to be confident in knowing God?

If you are confident in knowing that God is real, that the Bible is true, and that God loves and saves you, then some people might say, "You are arrogant. If you were humble, you'd be less sure. You wouldn't say that you know these things."

Is it arrogant to know something for sure? Not necessarily. We know the physical world is real. Would it be humbler to say we don't know? It's not a matter of being humble or proud. If we know it, we know it. Nobody calls us arrogant for knowing the physical world is real. The reality of the physical world is knowledge we can take as a given. Likewise, God's reality is knowledge we can take as a given. God is real. It's not arrogant to know this; it's just recognizing reality.

We know Abraham Lincoln was president. Would it be humbler to doubt this? No. Books and historians say Lincoln was president, so we believe it. In fact, we know it. We know by testimony that Lincoln was president. Knowing this with confidence does not mean we are proud. Likewise, we accept God's testimony that Jesus is his Son and that he raised Jesus from the dead. It's not arrogant to know this; it's just recognizing reality.

We know fire burns flesh. Would it be humbler to be unsure about this? Suppose I say, "Rather than arrogantly claiming to know that fire burns flesh, I encourage you to stick your hand in the flame and find out for yourself. I don't want to push my opinion on you." If I said this, you might say, "What kind of nutcase are you?" It's not arrogant to know that fire burns flesh. We know it by the experience of our faculties or by what others have said about their experience of fire. Likewise, a Christian knows that sin hurts and destroys. It's not arrogant to know this; it's just recognizing reality.

I know my wife loves me. Would it be humbler for me to worry and say, "Maybe she really hates me. Even though she promised at our wedding to love me 'till death do us part,' and even though she's been showering me with kindness and affection for decades, maybe she secretly hates me." No! I know my wife loves me. If you doubt whether your spouse loves you, that's not a sign of humility. It means either that you don't have a very trusting heart or that you don't have a very good spouse. I know by relating that my wife loves me—and I know God loves me. It's not arrogant to know this; it's just recognizing reality.

Confident knowledge is not necessarily arrogance. Some things you just know. So why do some people say you're arrogant if you claim to know things about God or about good and evil? It's mainly because we live in a society with a false division between facts and values. This mindset wrongly imagines that all claims of science and math are objective truth, while all claims of religion and morality are subjective opinion.

In this view, it's not at all arrogant to know something about science or math. If I say I know the moon orbits the earth, people won't say, "How can you be so arrogant?" If I say I know 3 + 3 = 6, they won't say to me, "You are so arrogant! You should be more humble and consider the possibility that 3 + 3 = 5." People won't accuse me of arrogance for confidently knowing something from the realm of science or math, because they view science and math as facts, as matters of objective truth.

When it comes to religion and morality, however, I might be accused of arrogance for claiming to know. That's because there is a bad habit of assuming that religion and morality are matters of subjective opinion or personal taste. In this view, faith deals only with values, not facts. It's okay to have confident knowledge of facts but not of values. If something is just a matter of taste or opinion, then it's arrogant to insist that you know the truth and that everybody else also ought to regard it as true.

This false dichotomy, this mistaken way of dividing facts and values, overestimates the factuality of science and math, and underestimates the factuality of Christianity. The Christian faith is about facts, not personal opinions. If you take God to be real and the Bible to be true, you are dealing with facts, with reality, and you are not arrogant for knowing what you know. Knowing by science and math is no more real or objective or certain than knowing by faith. Science is a human set of models for explaining reality. Math is a human set of symbols for interpreting reality. Math and science are not pure reality itself but models and symbols that give us partial knowledge of reality. In some respects, the knowledge of God is more real and more objective than math. God is more real, unchanging, and permanent than anything else, so God as the object of knowledge is more objective than any other object. The Bible is God's Word expressed in human words, so no merely human symbols or models can give us the same level of accuracy and certainty as the Bible provides.

We must reject the fact-value dichotomy and realize that biblical truths about God and morality are facts, not mere values or opinions. When we understand this, we will recognize that it's not a matter of arrogance to say that we know God and his truth when we accept Jesus and the Bible. Granted, it's possible to be arrogant, to be surer of things than you should be. If you really don't know what you're talking about, it is foolish and arrogant to talk as though you do. But if you really do know God, your confidence is not necessarily arrogance.

Is it humbler to be skeptical? Some people think so. They equate humility with uncertainty. They say, "When it comes to God, I'm agnostic. I don't know. And nobody else knows either." Often they think they are humble in saying this. *Agnostic* comes from a Greek word; it sounds trendy and smart. But the Latin equivalent is *ignoramus*. That doesn't sound so trendy or smart. *Agnostic* sounds better than *ignoramus*, but the root meaning is the same: "I don't know." If you say, "I'm agnostic," are you humbly admitting that you're an ignoramus who doesn't know God? Or are you proudly boasting that you're a brilliant skeptic? You don't know, so nobody else can possibly know— and you're smart enough to know that! Some skeptical agnostics are very arrogant to assume that if they don't know something, nobody else could possibly know it either.

Humility is a virtue, but it's harmful to have a phony "humility" that insists nobody can know anything.

> What we suffer from today is humility in the wrong place... A man was meant to be doubtful about himself, but undoubting about the truth; this has been exactly reversed. Nowadays the part of a man that a man does assert is exactly the part he ought not to assert—himself... The new skeptic is so humble that he doubts if he can even learn... We are on the road to producing a race of man too mentally modest to believe in the multiplication table (G. K. Chesterton).

In recent years, postmodernism has spread the notion that nobody knows objective truth. People are too mentally modest to believe the truths of God or the basic facts of math, yet they're very sure that they want what they want when they want it. That's misplaced humility. We ought to be much more humble about our own desires and urges and our sense of how things ought to be, and a bit less humble about the facts that can be known if we pay attention to God. If we know God's truth, we can be confident without being arrogant.

Is it hateful intolerance to know Jesus is the way?

Jesus has plainly said that he is the ultimate truth, the only way to God. There is no other. Some object to this and say it's hateful intolerance to know Jesus is the only way.

But what is tolerance? Does tolerance mean we assume that everyone is equally right? No, in that case, there would be no need for tolerance. Tolerance is not the notion that all views are on the right track; tolerance is putting up with people even when we think they are on the wrong track. There is no need for tolerance except when there is sharp disagreement on important matters. In such cases, tolerance means that although we are convinced other people are badly mistaken about something, we try to persuade them in a kind and respectful manner, rather than forcing them to change or killing them if they refuse to change.

If you try peacefully to persuade people to change their minds and their conduct, you may sometimes be accused of "hate speech." But is that because you hate them, or because they hate you? You might tolerate them and even love them very much. In fact, the more you love them, the more you want them to change for the better and try to persuade them.

Tolerance is not approval or agreement; tolerance is gentleness and respect in spite of disagreement. Religious tolerance is not the notion that all religions are true and lead to God; religious tolerance is recognizing the differences among religions and at the same time loving those who differ from us. Indeed, a hallmark of true tolerance is that people of different religions can speak freely to one another and try to persuade each other.

Christians who try to persuade others to follow Jesus are sometimes accused of hate and intolerance, but how tolerant are people who tell followers of Jesus to shut up about him? Hindu David Frawley says, "In the modern world we must recognize a pluralism not only of races and cultures but also of religion, which means that Christianity is not the only way. Such religious hate statements should no longer be tolerated and the organizations promoting them should be challenged." Without asking whether it's true that Christ is the only way, he simply dismisses the claims of Christ as "religious hate statements." Mr. Tolerance insists that efforts to share Jesus as the only Savior "should no longer be tolerated." He is so tolerant that he's intolerant!

Frawley objects to Christian missions and evangelism:

There is only one God, one book, one saviour, one final prophet and so on. Most Christian missionaries try to get people to accept Christ as their personal saviour and Christianity in one form or another as the true faith for all humanity.

A religion that is pluralistic in nature like the Hindu cannot have such a conversion-based ideology. Hindus accept that there are many paths, so naturally they will not feel compelled to get everyone to abandon their own path and follow the Hindu path instead. In fact there is no one Hindu path but rather a variety of paths, with new paths coming into being every day.

Conversion is a sin against the Divine in man... As we move into a global age, let us set this messy business of conversion behind, along with the other superstitions of the Dark Ages.

We are all God. There is only one Self in all creatures. Who is there to convert and what could anyone be converted from? The soul is Divine... The soul cannot be saved. It is beyond gain and loss.

It sounds open-minded and tolerant to say all religions are true, but in the same breath, Christianity is said to be false. Christian teachings that all people should believe one Bible and one Savior are called "superstitions of the Dark Ages." God says, "You shall have no other gods before me," but Hindus flatly deny this. They honor various gods and goddesses and even say, "We are all God." But we're not God; we're human sinners. There are not many gods and goddesses worthy of worship; there is one God. There are not many paths to God; there's one. His name is Jesus.

If you think all religions work equally well, you are not thinking like a Christian. You are thinking like a Hindu or a humanist. Hindu doctrine teaches that all religions are true because everything is God, including you. Humanist doctrine teaches that all religions may be "true" as useful myths only because all religions are false as fact. There is no God, say the humanists, but they grant that religious stories and rituals may help some people. If you believe that there is no God (like an atheistic humanist) or that everything is God (like a pantheistic Hindu), you can claim that all religions belong on the same level. But if the God of the Bible is real, and if Jesus died to pay for the sins of the world and then rose from the dead, you must believe it and do all you can to persuade others to believe it.

Is it hateful to say, "Jesus is the only way of salvation?" No. It's hateful to say, "We don't need Jesus for salvation." Consider these words from the Bible:

The blood of Jesus, his Son, purifies us from all sin. If we claim to be without sin, we deceive ourselves and the truth is not in us. If we confess our sins, he is faithful and just and will forgive us our sins and purify us from all unrighteousness. If we claim we have not sinned, we make him out to be a liar ...

Anyone who does not believe God has made him out to be a liar, because he has not believed the testimony God has given about his Son. And this is the testimony: God has given us eternal life, and this life is in his Son. He who has the Son has life; he who does not have the Son of God does not have life (1 John 1:7-10; 5:9-12).

If you say, "I don't need Jesus," you are saying, "God, you're a liar. When you say I'm a sinner, you lie. When you say you sent your Son to die for my sin, you lie. When you say anyone who does not have the Son of God does not have life, you lie."

It's hateful to call God a liar, and it's hateful to call Jesus a liar. Jesus said, "I am the way and the truth and the life. No one comes to the Father except through me" (John 14:6). If you say there are many ways to God, you are calling Jesus a liar.

Is it hateful to know Jesus is the only way? No, it is loving toward Jesus to believe what he says, and it is loving toward other people to let them know what you know: that Jesus is the only way to eternal life. What's really hateful is to pretend there are other ways for people to be made right with God when there aren't. The most loving thing I can do for others is to introduce them to Jesus as the only one who can make them right with God and give them eternal life.

Is it judgmental to say others are wrong?

Many people think that being judgmental is a terrible thing, and they think it's judgmental for Christians to say we are right to believe the Bible and others are wrong to reject it. But is it always judgmental for a person to say someone else is wrong?

Is it judgmental for a mother to say that 8 x 7 = 56 and that her child is wrong to say that 8 x 7 = 54? The mother is not being cruel, mean, harsh, or judgmental. She is simply showing the child's error and teaching the truth.

Is it judgmental for a scientist to say the earth orbits the sun and to say earlier scientists were wrong to say the sun orbited the earth? In one sense, of course, it's a judgment, but not a nasty, mean judgment. It's simply recognizing that one view is right and the other is wrong.

Is it judgmental for a doctor to say that penicillin will cure an infection and that a patient is wrong to believe snake oil will help? It's not wrongly judgmental to say that. We all have to make judgments. We need to make right judgments. Penicillin cures infections; snake oil doesn't. A good doctor will say so, not to be judgmental, but to help a patient.

As a believer in Jesus and the Bible, you can know non-believers are wrong and you are right without being wrongly judgmental. You can make a right judgment about truth without having an eager-to-condemn, judgmental attitude toward other people and wanting the worst for them.

Can you really know you have eternal life?

Knowing by faith that you are saved is considered rare or even bad by some church traditions. Official Roman Catholic theology says that most Christians should not be sure of their own salvation. A favored few can know their eternal destiny, but the rest can only hope, wait, and work. But according to the Bible, God wants Christians to know: "I write these things to you who believe in the name of the Son of God so that you may know that you have eternal life" (1 John 5:13). God wants you to know not just eternal truths about him and historical facts about Jesus, but he also wants you to know that you belong to him, that you have been forgiven, and that your future glory is secure and certain. The Heidelberg Catechism says,

> True faith is not only a sure knowledge by which I hold as true all that God has revealed to us in Scripture; it is also a wholehearted trust, which the Holy Spirit creates in me by the gospel, that God has freely granted, not only to others but to me also, forgiveness of sins, eternal righteousness, and salvation. These are gifts of sheer grace, granted solely by Christ's merit.

When you know the gospel and trust Jesus, you can know that you have eternal life.

Is faith ever unclear or unsure?

We can know divine truths by faith and know our own salvation by faith. Does this mean real faith is always absolutely clear and certain? Does this mean that if we don't understand doctrinal details clearly and precisely, or if we're not 100 percent sure about something, then we don't have real faith? No, it's possible to have some confusion and uncertainty but still have real faith and real knowledge.

Jesus often said, "You of little faith" (Matthew 6:30, 8:26, 14:31, 16:8, 17:20). Little faith is different from no faith. Many of us are people of little faith. Our faith knowledge is sometimes vague; there are many things we need to understand in clearer detail. Our faith knowledge is sometimes weak; we lack full confidence in what we know. Little faith might not see clearly or know surely, but though small, it is real. Even small faith may hold real knowledge. We know things with varying degrees of clarity and certainty. We might be unclear on some points, yet have real knowledge. We might be unsure at times, yet know to at least some degree.

Little faith can seek increasing clarity and certainty. The range and precision of our knowledge should continue to grow so that we have not just small, vague knowledge but vast, clear knowledge. The certainty of our knowledge should grow so that we have not just weak, trembling assurance but strong, bold assurance.

Meanwhile, don't be discouraged if your knowledge is still small and your assurance is still weak. If you know that Jesus saves and you go to Jesus—even with hesitations, even with uncertainties—he will surely save you. If you sometimes have questions or difficulties understanding the Bible but you keep going to God's Word, then you have a genuine faith in God's truth and his promises. As you keep searching, your little faith will grow. God will make your knowledge of him clearer and surer.

Why do we need faith if we have knowledge?

Some people say, "If you know it, you don't need faith." But knowledge is not just a thing you store in your mind like you store a tool on a shelf. Knowledge can decay or be lost. Your social setting, actions, and heart can affect your mind and change what you previously thought you knew. Knowledge of God requires ongoing faith because sometimes you get into a negative social setting, or slip into bad behavior, or have heart struggles, and your knowledge of God will collapse without faith.

Your *social setting* shapes your knowledge. Instead of being among Christians, you may be among people who don't believe what you believe. What you knew as long as you were in a godly social setting will fade unless you have the commitment and the knowledge that come through faith. Faith will keep you believing the things you know to be true, even in a hostile setting; and faith will draw you to the church community that supports your knowledge of God.

Your *actions* shape your knowledge. Sinful actions make it harder to believe; good actions make it easier to believe. Sinning is like splattering mud on the windshield of your car: the more you sin, the more your vision is blocked. If faith motivates you to keep acting as God directs, you will continue to see clearly instead of constantly splattering mud on your windshield and making it harder to see and to know the things of God. When you sin, faith will send you to Christ for cleansing, and this will enable you to see truth rather than being blinded by your sin.

Your *heart* shapes your knowledge. If your heart is divided or corrupted, any knowledge of God that you had will fragment or fail—unless faith gets the heart back on track. By faith the heart trusts and longs for God and gets back in tune with God, and the mind is then able to hold on to what it knows about God.

We tend to view knowledge as firmer than faith, and faith as weaker than knowledge, but it turns out to be the opposite: knowledge depends on faith. We gain knowledge by faith and maintain it by faith. Without faith, knowledge of God tends to slip away from us. If you lack faith in God, Satan can overthrow your knowledge at any time.

> Reason may win truths; without Faith she will retain them just so long as Satan pleases. There is nothing we cannot be made to believe or disbelieve. If we wish to be rational, not now and then, but constantly, we must pray for the gift of Faith, for the power to go on believing not in the teeth of reason but in the teeth of lust and terror and jealousy and boredom and indifference that which reason, authority, and experience, or all three, have once delivered to us for truth. (C. S. Lewis)

Satan can make you believe or disbelieve just about anything. How can a man who is totally male in his anatomy and chromosomes and has fathered several children declare, "I am really a woman?" How can other people consider such a man to be a woman? It turns out people can be made to believe just about anything, even when it totally contradicts biology and all observable facts. Without faith in the true and living God, knowledge is not so firm and solid as we might think. Strong faith in God's truth makes knowledge strong; otherwise, all knowledge is weak and vulnerable. Faith is not the enemy of reason; faith is the friend that keeps reason strong and clear so that we can hold on-to knowledge when all sorts of irrational forces attack what we know. In our most rational moments, we can see that God is re-al, the Bible is true, and Jesus is Lord. When we think about the claims of Christianity clearly and logically, we find them solid and well substantiated. But when our desires or fears or boredom kick in, Christianity seems unreal to us. When Satan turns up the heat, what seemed certain can suddenly seem ridiculous.

Why do we need faith if we have knowledge? Because faith is the key to knowing many things in the first place, and faith is what gives knowledge its strength and staying power when irra-tional urges and demonic deceptions attack our knowledge.

Is it irrational to believe despite contrary evidence?

Sometimes Christians are confronted with things that seem to contradict Christianity. Should you continue to believe even in the face of contrary evidence? Or should you follow the latest evidence wherever it seems to lead? In that case, if the evidence supports Christianity, it's rational for you to believe it. If there seems to be strong evidence against it, it's rational to reject it. And if there seems to be about equal evidence for and against, it's rational to say, "I don't know" and wait for more evidence one way or the other. With that approach, it might seem irra-tional to continue believing despite contrary evidence. However, it's not necessarily irrational to continue believing strongly.

Would it be irrational to believe you did not commit a crime even if lots of evidence seemed to point to your guilt? If you knew you didn't commit a murder and somebody was trying to frame you with a lot of evidence indicating that you did it, would it be rational for you to say, "I have to go with the evi-dence. I did it." No! Evidence cannot change your mind about something you know for yourself. You didn't do it. You know you didn't do it. It would not be rational to go against what you know just because some evidence seemed to point in the other direction.

The same is true if you've come to know God. Once God has revealed himself to you and showed you your sin and your need of a Savior, once God has implanted his life in you and given you personal trust in the living Lord Jesus, it is rational to continue believing strongly in your Lord even if various things arise that seem contrary to your faith. You know what you know, and no amount of additional evidence can change what you know to be true.

Would it be irrational to believe in a dear, wise, capable friend even if things happened that you couldn't understand or explain? You know your friend has excellent character and always wants what is best for you. He does some things you can't understand, but you know that he's smart and that he loves you, so you continue trusting. It is rational to say, "I can't figure out why he's doing things this way, but I trust him."

So it is with God. Once you come to know him as Father, to know that he loves you, that he has your best interest in mind, that his wisdom and his ways are too great and mysterious for you always to understand, then you trust him even when evidence seems to point in a different direction. Believing "evidence" rather than believing God might show disloyalty, not rationality. God might say to you, "You should have known me better." If some stranger were to accuse my wife of something horrible, should I just believe that stranger the moment they present a bit of evidence? That would not be fair to my wife. I know her. She's loved me for decades. It would take a lot more than a few shreds of evidence from a stranger to overturn everything I know of my wife and destroy our entire relationship.

It is sometimes wise and rational to believe strongly in a person despite some evidence to the contrary. Knowledge by material analysis is not always better than knowledge by personal acquaintance. In material analysis, you examine a thing that you can measure, control, and dissect. In personal acquaintance, you understand through interaction what a person is thinking and feeling, and how that person regards you. This kind of knowledge depends on the other person's revelation to you and on your receptivity to what he is revealing of himself. You can't know much about me by killing me, dissecting me, and cutting up my brain. You would learn a few things about my anatomy, but you would learn very little about what makes me the person I am. You'd learn a lot more by spending time with me and interacting with me than by trying to analyze me. You could know very little about me if I refused to reveal anything about myself or if you refused to pay attention to anything I said. That is certainly the case with God. We know nothing of God unless he shows himself to us and unless we're receptive to what he shows us. But if God does communicate his reality to us and we come to know him through personal acquaintance, then "evidence" gained from analysis won't count against him.

It makes sense to believe strongly in the Lord even when we can't make sense of contrary evidence. Our minds are too small to figure God out. The Lord says, "For as the heavens are higher than the earth, so are my ways higher than your ways and my thoughts than your thoughts" (Isaiah 55:0). If God could fit into that small space inside your skull, if your little brain could figure out the infinite God, then he wouldn't be God. God's ways are far beyond ours. Faith is very rational when it says, "Lord, I am like a little child. I'm not going to concern myself with things too great for me. I'm going to trust that you know what you're doing because you've shown yourself to be a loving and faithful Father to me." That's not irrational; it's not turning your brain off. It's realism about who God is in comparison to us.

Here's another reason it makes sense to believe despite contrary evidence: Satan will surely bring contrary evidence in an attempt to lead us away from God and his truth. "For false Christs and false prophets will appear and perform great signs and miracles to deceive even the elect—if that were possible" (Matthew 24:24). God's elect, God's chosen, cannot be deceived or lose their salvation, but if it were possible and if it depended strictly on strong evidence, the evidence from Satan would be more than enough to make everyone stop believing. Of course there will be evidence and arguments against the truth of the

Christian faith! Of course that evidence will seem strong! Satan is constantly manufacturing and presenting such evidence. It is not rational to change your mind every time the enemy of your soul sends new "evidence" to deceive you.

Faith involves knowledge by acquaintance. It makes sense to believe in God, to know his reality and trust his goodness despite contrary "evidence," because personal encounter outweighs impersonal analysis. When you become personally acquainted with God, you're not just analyzing evidence or propositions or things; you are in relationship with the living Lord. You also know that a different sort of personality is out to ruin that relationship, so you remain alert to Satan and his schemes. You do not allow Satan to manipulate "evidence" in a way that undermines your knowledge of God and your confidence in him.

In a Nutshell

Is it arrogant to be confident in knowing God? Not necessarily. God wants us to be clear and sure in our knowledge of him. We can be confident of God without being proud of ourselves.

Is it hateful intolerance to know Jesus is the way? No. It's hateful toward God to say Jesus is not the only way; that is calling God a liar. It's also hateful toward people not to help them find the one way to eternal life.

Is it judgmental to say others are wrong? Not necessarily. We may simply be stating the facts, and we may be stating those facts in order to help others discover more truth.

Can you really know you have eternal life? Yes. God wants you to know.

Is faith ever unclear or unsure? Yes. We may have faith that is real but small, faith that is genuine but not perfectly clear or fully certain. Sometimes we have to pray like a man who said to Jesus, "Lord, I believe. Help my unbelief" (Mark 9:24).

Why do we need faith if we have knowledge? Knowledge can be twisted or lost. Satan can get us to believe just about anything if we don't have faith and commitment. Our minds can change very easily without faith to receive God's ongoing help.

Is it irrational to believe despite contrary evidence? It is rational to continue believing if we know God by personal acquaintance and find him trustworthy. God's ways are not our ways. Besides, Satan is eager to feed us misleading evidence. It is rational to trust God and to refuse Satan's ploys.

Having faced these questions about knowing by faith, we can say with the apostle John, "We know that the Son of God has come and has given us understanding, so that we may know him who is true" (1 John 5:20).

Chapter 20

Seeking God's Face

I do not know God nearly as well as I would like to know him. Sometimes my sense of God can get so dim that I wonder whether I know him at all. I've studied the Bible a lot, and I know many things about God, but I still don't know God himself the way I want to know him.

What I know of God can seem secondhand. God can seem more like a set of concepts I've picked up from others than a living, fascinating friend whom I know personally. I wish I could say God walks with me and talks with me on a constant basis, but sometimes I feel as though I'm walking alone in silence. I believe that God is there and that he is not silent, but all too often I do not hear his voice or perceive his presence.

Oh, there are times—precious times—when I do sense God close at hand, filling me with his life and his love, but those times are not nearly as frequent or as intense as I would like. There are times—precious times—when my prayers seem to be really connecting and I sense God listening and answering, but there are also times when my prayer time feels like I'm talking to the ceiling. There are times—precious times—when the Bible stirs my soul, and I sense the Spirit of God speaking to my spirit. But there are also times when I can't even focus on the page in front of me. I get drowsy or distracted, and reading the Bible seems like a toilsome chore, not a lively conversation. Even when I'm able to concentrate and really think about what the Bible says, my head may just pick up more facts without my heart getting any closer to God.

The worst times of all are those terrible times when I willfully sin, when I think or say or do something I know is wrong. If I truly sensed God beside me and within me, how could I offend him to his face? When I sin, I am acting as though God is absent. I am acting in unbelief. When I give in to temptation, it's not just because of my weakness or the power of the temptation. It's because in that moment I'm not experiencing God and don't have a clear, vivid sense of him and don't hold true to the fact that he is present with me.

It hurts to admit that I experience less of God than I long for. It hurts when God seems more like a distant concept than a nearby Father. It hurts not to know God as well as I'd like. Being a preacher makes it hurt even more. If I am beset by the feeling that I don't know God as well as I should, how dare I introduce others to him? When I speak about the joy and wonder of knowing Jesus, am I advertising more than what I've tasted myself? As a messenger for God, I want to speak from the overflow of my heart, not from dryness and thirst.

Usually I keep such thoughts to myself. My calling is to proclaim Jesus and to build faith in him, not to talk about my personal experience (or lack of it). You need Jesus more than you need to know about the feebleness of my faith. The Bible is true and the Lord is wonderful, regardless of what I happen to feel at a given moment. I would not bother telling of my own thirst in relation to God, except that I know many others are also thirsty and have much the same longing for God that I have.

I want to share the deepest desire of my heart for myself and for you. My deepest desire is to know God and grow closer to him. My name is David, and I echo my namesake, the biblical King David. In Psalm 27 David says, "One thing I ask of he Lord, this is what I seek: that I may dwell in the house of the Lord all the days of my life, to gaze upon the beauty of the Lord and to seek him in his temple." Then David says to God, "My heart says of you, 'Seek his face!' Your face, Lord, I will seek." For years that verse has been a guiding star for me: "Your face, Lord, I will seek." I urge you also to seek his face and his beauty.

Do you want to know God better? Do you crave a closer relationship with him? If so, I speak to you as a fellow traveler, not as one who has arrived at the destination. I am not way out ahead of you in my relationship with God, shouting back some instructions on how you can get as close to God as I am. I do relate to God as my Father, and I treasure my relationship to him more than anything in the world, but I still don't know God nearly as well as I would like to know him.

Seeking More

If you're like me—if you know just enough of God to want more of him—then here's the question: How should we deal with this craving? Should we tell ourselves not to want too much or expect too much? Should we try to get used to going through life without knowing God much better than we presently do? Or should we desire more and pursue more and expect more?

I'm convinced we should seek more. In some ways, it might be easier to settle for less. It might be less frustrating not to get our hopes too high. It might be easier just to settle for believing we're forgiven, reading our Bible, and going to heaven someday. But I want more. I don't just want forgiveness; I want *friendship* with God. I don't just want to read about the peace of God that surpasses understanding (Philippians 4:7); I want to *feel* that peace. I don't just want to read about being "filled with inexpressible and glorious joy" (1 Peter 1:8); I want that joy to saturate my whole being. I don't just want to read about God's love being poured out in our hearts by the Holy Spirit (Romans 5:5); I want to *experience* that outpouring of love. I don't just want to read that "the Lord is good" (Psalm 100:5); I want to "*taste and see* that the Lord is good" (Psalm 34:8). I don't just want to someday enjoy being with Christ in heaven; I want to enjoy his nearness *now*—as much as he's willing to grant. It might be easier to settle for less, but I can't. My heart says, "Seek his face," so I cry, "Your face, Lord, I will seek."

As I seek God's face, there's a verse in the Bible that fills me with longing. Exodus 33:11 says, "The Lord would speak to Moses face to face, as a man speaks with his friend." That's what I want: to be face to face with God, to hear his voice clearly and directly, to communicate the way close friends do. I know that Moses was unique and that God revealed himself to Moses in stunning experiences that are duplicated seldom if ever. The Bible says, "Since then, no prophet has risen in Israel like Moses, whom the Lord knew face to face" (Deuteronomy 34:10). Even so, since the coming of Jesus, there are many respects in which followers of Jesus today can know the Lord better than Moses did. Moses did not have Jesus' full teaching; Jesus had not yet died and risen; the Holy Spirit had not come upon God's people as fully as he would later do; so there were some things that Moses could foresee only dimly. Living in the light of Christ, why should we settle for having any less of God in our life than Moses had?

The Pursuit of God

A. W. Tozer, a pastor from an earlier generation, wrote a spiritual classic called *The Pursuit of God*. Tozer believed in accurate Bible teaching but said such teaching is not enough.

> There is today no lack of Bible teachers to set forth correctly the principles of the doctrines of Christ, but too many of these seem satisfied to teach the fundamentals of the faith year after year, strangely unaware that there is in their ministry no manifest Presence, nor anything unusual in their personal lives. They minister constantly to believers who feel within their breasts a longing which their teaching simply does not satisfy... They want to taste, to touch with their hearts, to see with their inner eyes the wonder that is God.

But in many churches, that's not happening. "In its stead," said Tozer, "are programs, methods, organizations and a world of nervous activities which occupy time and attention but can never satisfy the longing of the heart."

We need God. We don't just need religious activities; we need God himself. Tozer declared,

The world is perishing for lack of the knowledge of God and the church is famishing for want of His presence. The instant cure of most of our religious ills would be to enter the Presence in spiritual experience, to become suddenly aware that we are in God and God is in us. This would lift us out of our pitiful narrowness and cause our hearts to be enlarged.

This is especially urgent for those of us who are leaders and pastors. Are we real worshipers and friends of God, or are we just experts on theology? Tozer put it well:

The scribe tells us what he has read, and the prophet tells us what he has seen... Between the scribe who has read and the prophet who has seen there is a difference as wide as the sea. We are overrun today with orthodox scribes, but the prophets, where are they? The hard voice of the scribe sounds over evangelicalism, but the church waits for the tender voice of the saint who has penetrated the veil and has gazed with inward eye on the wonder that is God.

Those words drive me to my knees. I pray that God will forgive me when I've settled for mere logic and research and biblical analysis without seeking his face and desiring his presence. I pray that God will forgive me when I have failed others by speaking with the hard voice of a scribe who is better at arguing than at worshiping and loving. I pray that God will fill me to overflowing with the living, loving Person of his Holy Sprit. I pray that God will show me more and more of Christ. I pray that I may truly be in tune with the heart of my heavenly Father, that I may experience God's love for me, and that I may love God more truly. I pray that I may speak to others with the warmth and power that flows out of friendship with God. I pray that you too will seek God's face and relate to Jesus more directly and vibrantly.

God's Word encourages you and me in our desire to know him better. The apostle Paul says, "I consider everything a loss compared to the surpassing greatness of knowing Christ Jesus my Lord... I want to know Christ." After expressing that intense desire, Paul adds, "Not that I have already obtained all this or have already been made perfect, but I press on" (Philippians 3:8,10,12). Paul had amazing encounters with Christ and direct revelations from the Lord, but even Paul did not know Christ as well as he wanted. If you and I have come to know Christ at all, it's reason to rejoice, but at the same time it rouses a hunger to seek his face and know him more.

Don't Settle For Less

Do you want to know God more? When you hear the Bible say, "The Lord would speak with Moses face to face, as a man speaks with his friend," how do you respond? Does something inside you long for face to face friendship with the Almighty? When we look at the way Moses related to God, we find that Moses wanted as much of God as the Lord was willing to give.

While Moses was up on Mount Sinai getting the Ten Commandments and other revelations from God, the Israelite people were making themselves a golden calf to worship. They turned away from the Lord who rescued them from slavery, and they bowed down to a hunk of junk. This angered the Lord, and he threatened to wipe them all out. But Moses pleaded for God not to destroy them, and God relented. The Lord said he would not destroy the people. Rather, he would send an angel along with them to give them victory in their struggles and make a place for them in the promised land. God would do all this for them, but he said that he himself would not go with them.

Suppose God told you, "I am not going to destroy you for your sins. What's more, I'll make sure an angel deals with any obstacles in your path, and I'll make sure you get to heaven in the end." That's a better deal than any of us deserve, so a lot of people might gladly settle for that. It's tempting to say, "Wow! Sounds wonderful! Who could ask for more?"

Moses asked for more. It wasn't enough for him and his fellow Israelites to escape destruction or to have an angel protector or to win victories or to arrive at the place God promised. They couldn't bear to hear God say, "I'll do these things for you, but

I'm not going with you on the way. I'll send an angel, but I'm not coming." When God said that, Moses and all the Israelites started crying. Moses didn't want to take even one more step on the journey if God would not go with them. Forgiveness, an angel, and a prosperous future might be nice, but what are these worth without fellowship with God?

Moses said to the Lord, "You have been telling me, 'Lead these people,' but you have not let me know whom you will send with me. You have said, 'I know you by name and you have found favor with me.' If you are pleased with me, teach me your ways so that I may know you and continue to find favor with you. Remember that this nation is your people."

The Lord replied, "My Presence will go with you, and I will give you rest."

Then Moses said to him, "If your Presence does not go with us, do not send us up from here…"

And the Lord said to Moses, "I will do the very thing you have asked, because I am pleased with you and I know you by name (Exodus 33:12-17).

Moses wouldn't settle for being forgiven and helped by a God who would stay at a distance and remain largely anonymous. Moses eagerly sought to know God and to experience his favor. Moses didn't want to go anywhere without God; he wanted God beside him and the Israelites at all times.

Does God's Presence mean that much to you? Or do you settle for less? Are you satisfied as long as you're forgiven and bound for the Promised Land, even if you have little or no sense of God's presence in your life? Don't settle for that! Keep pleading for God's favor and presence the way Moses did.

Show Me Your Glory

Moses would not settle for less. He wanted to have as much of God as the Lord was willing to give him. He wanted to know as much of God as the Lord was willing to show him. He wanted this for the benefit of all God's people, but he also wanted direct, personal encounter. Moses must have been overjoyed when God promised his continuing presence. But even then Moses kept asking for more. He blurted out, "Now show me your glory."

What a stupendous request! Moses had seen many of God's miracles, heard many of God's promises, and experienced God's presence, but now he wanted the ultimate: a display of the vast splendor and being of God. And God didn't mind being asked. When God shows us favor and gives us something of himself, he likes it when we keep asking for more. As Jesus put it, "Whoever has will be given more, and he will have an abundance" (Matthew 13:12). Moses had received much, but he kept seeking more, and God was pleased to reveal more—but not everything. When Moses said, "Show me your glory,' the Lord said,

> "I will cause all my goodness to pass in front of you, and I will proclaim my name, the Lord, in your presence. I will have mercy on whom I will have mercy, and I will have compassion on whom I will have compassion. But," he said, "you cannot see my face, for no one may see me and live."
>
> Then the Lord said, "There is a place near me where you may stand on a rock. When my glory passes by, I will put you in a cleft in the rock and cover you with my hand till I have passed by. Then I will remove my hand and you will see my back; but my face must not be seen" (Exodus 33:19-23).

No mere human could survive a full vision of God's glory. In order to reveal himself to us without destroying us, God must shelter us from his full glory and allow us to catch a glimpse of his back but not his face, of his afterglow but not his direct brilliance. Even that indirect, partial encounter is enough to transform our lives and make us radiant. When Moses came from God back to the people, his face shone with dazzling brightness.

There is a great mystery here. The Bible says Moses "saw him who is invisible" (Hebrews 11:27). What does it mean to see the invisible? Exodus 33:11 says, "The Lord would speak to Moses face to face, as a man speaks with his friend," but just nine verses later, in Exodus 33:20, God tells Moses, "You cannot see my face, for no one may see me and live." How can the Bible speak of being face to face with God and then say that no one can see God's face and live? Here's what I think it means: it's possible for us to be face to face with God in the sense of personal fellowship but not in the sense that we see everything about him. We can't look God over and size him up the way we might a fellow human. God is too vast, splendid, mighty, and mysterious for that. The sheer weight of his majesty would crush us.

Still, the fact that no one can see God's face in the ultimate sense should not prevent us from seeking his face in the sense of getting to know him better and experience more of him. Let's not stifle our yearning for God by saying, "Well, we're not Moses. He was different. Nothing like that is possible for me." God has revealed far greater glory in Christ than what he revealed to Moses on Mount Sinai. When the Bible compares God's revelation to Moses with the revelation in Christ, it says, "What was glorious has no glory now in comparison with the surpassing glory" (2 Corinthians 3:10).

There's a sense in which I already know the Lord better than Moses did. I might not hear God's voice audibly or have such direct vision—and I do long for clearer, more direct encounters—but I still know God's revelation in Christ in ways that Moses did not. The Bible says, "No one has ever seen God, but God the One and Only [that is, Jesus] has made him known" (John 1:18). After Jesus ascended to heaven, God gave his Holy Spirit to his people in richer measure than he did in earlier times. God's Word says, "Now the Lord is the Spirit, and where the Spirit (708) 570-0685of the Lord is, there is freedom. And we all, with unveiled faces, beholding the glory of the Lord, are being changed into his likeness from one degree of glory to another; for this comes from the Lord, who is the Spirit" (2 Corinthians 3:17-18 RSV).

God puts limits to what we can see of him and know of him in this life, but how many of us are anywhere near those limits?

Could our relationship with God be less distant and more direct if only we wanted it more and prayed for it more urgently?

Seeing His Face

Jesus says, "Blessed are the pure in heart, for they will see God" (Matthew 5:8). To see God, we must be pure in heart. What does this mean? It means to be clean of sin, but even more it means to have a single-minded, undivided desire for God. When God is our supreme desire, when nothing matters to us compared to knowing the Lord, then we are pure in heart, and we will see God. Before we see him, we must want him.

If we are discouraged by how dimly we know God, let us seek him all the more urgently. And when God blesses and refreshes us with a sense of his nearness and a taste of his glory, let's not settle for that. Let's keep seeking and praying for more.

Let's seek for more already in this life, and let's pray more urgently for Jesus to come again and establish his perfect new creation. Already God loves us who belong to Jesus as friends and dear children, but when Jesus returns, it will be even better. "When he appears, we shall be like him, for we shall see him as he is" (1 John 3:2). For now, "We live by faith, not by sight" (2 Corinthians 5:7), but we can ask God to reveal more of himself to the eyes of faith, and each of us can pray, "O Lord, haste the day when my faith shall be sight."

So seek for God to display more of his glory right here, right now, and at the same time pray that Jesus will come soon and display his full glory for all to see. "What we see now is like a dim image in a mirror; then we shall see face-to-face. What I know now is only partial; then it will be complete—as complete as God's knowledge of me" (1 Corinthians 13:12 TEV). In the Lord's new creation, his people "will see his face... They will not need the light of a lamp or the light of the sun, for the Lord God will give them light. And they will reign for ever and ever" (Revelation 22:4-5).

Acknowledgements

Much of the material in this book was first communicated in personal conversations, radio talks, and video presentations. I have tried to think clearly and speak plainly, without scholarly lingo or footnotes. Of the many sources I have drawn upon, some of the most helpful are: G. K. Chesterton, Stephen Evans, Phillip Johnson, C. S. Lewis, Alvin Plantinga, and A. W. Tozer.

Over the years, Back to God Ministries, Family of Faith Church, and Christian Leaders Institute have supported my ministry and provided me with opportunities to interact with many questioners. I am grateful.

Christian Leaders Institute

Christian Leaders Institute provides
free online ministry training worldwide.

www.christianleadersinstitute.org

Made in the USA
Middletown, DE
23 January 2017